SHARKS

▼ Sharks are the ocean's top predators. This blue shark has the typical streamlined shape.

KFK KINGFISHER KNOWLEDGE

SHARKS

Miranda Smith

Foreword by
Valerie Taylor

KINGFISHER

KINGFISHER

First published 2008 by Kingfisher
an imprint of Macmillan Children's Books
a division of Macmillan Publishers Limited
20 New Wharf Road, London N1 9RR
Basingstoke and Oxford
www.panmacmillan.com

Associated companies throughout the world

Consultant: David Burnie

ISBN 978 0 7534 1605 1

1 2 3 4 5 6 7 8 9
1TR/1107/TWP/MA(MA)/130ENSOMA/F

A CIP catalogue record for this book is available from the British Library.

Printed in Singapore

Contents

Foreword   6

CHAPTER 1
MEET THE SHARK   7

The shark family   8–9
Inside a shark   10–11
Giving birth   12–13
Ancient sharks   14–15
Record breakers   16–17
Hammerheads   18–19
Rarest of all   20–21
Near relatives   22–23
Migration   24–25
Open ocean   26–27
Deep-sea hunters   28–29
On the reef   30–31
Summary   32

CHAPTER 2
SHARK ATTACK! 33

Teeth	34–35
Targeting prey	36–37
Hunting in packs	38–39
Man-eaters	40–41
Giant filter-feeders	42–43
Bottom-feeders	44–45
Summary	46

CHAPTER 3
SHARKS AND PEOPLE 47

Myths and legends	48–49
Shark tales	50–51
Threats to sharks	52–53
Getting up close	54–55
Conservation	56–57
Summary	58
Glossary	59–61
Index	62–63
Acknowledgements	64

▼ A blue shark is filmed in the sea off the coast of California, USA.

GO FURTHER...
INFORMATION PANEL KEY:

websites and further reading

career paths

places to visit

Foreword

The shark is a rare and beautiful animal, so perfect in design that it has not changed in millions of years. It is also an animal I've worked with for most of my adult life. On page 54, you can see me in the water with a whitetip reef shark. My husband, cameraman Ron Taylor, and I have made a successful career by specializing in filming sharks. You can read about shark movies on pages 50–51.

Probably our best-known footage was shot for the film *Jaws*, but my most dramatic moment happened while working on a documentary called *Amazing Animals*. We were filming 100km off the coast of San Diego, southwestern USA. We had used bait to attract dozens of blue sharks, just like the ones on pages 26–27. Perhaps because there were so many of them, they seemed unusually excited; I was busy punching them away when I felt a thump to my left leg. Looking down, I saw a good-sized shark with my leg in his mouth. I grabbed his nose and tried to push him off. On my fourth hit I finally saw the teeth pull back from my leg. I didn't feel pain or fear – just annoyance that the shark had been so persistent. Blood clouded the water. I tried to stop it but my middle finger sank from sight into the wound. 'I'm going to bleed to death,' I thought. I tried without success to pull the thick neoprene of my wetsuit over the gash. Then someone was helping me through the sharks back to the boat – I don't remember too well. The coastguard, already in the air, arrived in minutes. I was taken by helicopter to hospital, where it took 300 stitches to sew my leg back together. Yes, it did become painful – very painful – and it still gives me trouble, but my own quick thinking saved my leg. I have been bitten twice more, but not badly. If I make the decision to enter the domain of a predator and things go wrong, the fault is entirely mine. Mercifully, as you will see on pages 40–41, shark attacks are relatively rare.

Another of my most memorable shark encounters was with a species that is rarely seen – the great hammerhead. (You can read about hammerheads on pages 18–19.) To hang in the open water and watch a 6m-long shark emerge from the gloom, its enormous head swinging back and forth, has one's heart jumping. To have the same beast swim directly towards you and look you over – not once, but many times – makes you feel exactly what you are: an out-of-place earthling in an alien environment. There was no threat, just curiosity, but it was still unsettling. The shark was so very big, with such long, sharp teeth, and her expressionless eyes seemed to be boring into mine. Eventually, curiosity satisfied, the hammerhead disappeared just as silently as she had arrived.

I hope that one day you have the opportunity to get up close to sharks in the water as I do. In the meantime, you can observe them and learn about them by reading this book. As you will read on pages 56–57, spreading knowledge about sharks is one of the most important ways that we can help to look after them.

Valerie Taylor

Valerie Taylor, shark expert and marine conservationist

Meet the shark

A powerful and determined hunter scything through the waves, its jaws widening to reveal terrifying, razor-sharp teeth. Is this the picture that springs to mind when the word 'shark' is mentioned? Despite their reputation, most sharks are harmless and shark attacks are very rare. Sharks probably have more to fear from humans than vice versa. Of all the animals that have existed on earth, there are not many that have been around as long, or survived as well, as the shark. The ancestors of this skilful predator were swimming in the oceans 450 million years ago, 220 million years before the age of the dinosaurs even began. Today, there are around 375 species of shark. Sharks are found all over the world, from tropical seas to cold polar waters, and from the ocean depths to estuaries and rivers.

An oceanic whitetip shark swims in the tropical seas off Hawaii, accompanied by striped pilot-fish.

The shark family

A typical shark has a sleek, streamlined shape. Its body tapers off at both ends, allowing the shark to glide smoothly through the water without using a lot of energy. Most sharks never stop swimming and can only move forwards. It also never sleeps. It has superb senses that it uses to avoid predators and find prey. And a shark has no bones – instead, its skeleton is made of cartilage, a tough, flexible tissue made of fibres.

All shapes and sizes

Sharks range in size from the massive whale shark to tiny pygmy sharks (see pages 16–17). They vary greatly in shape as well. Angel sharks and wobbegongs have flattened bodies, hammerheads have unusually wide heads, while frilled sharks are long and eel-like. Some sharks, such as mako and tiger sharks, are swift hunters. Others, including the zebra bullhead shark, search the seabed for crabs and clams. And some, such as the basking shark, filter plankton from the water.

eye has nictitating membrane (inner eyelid)

mouth is under snout

gill slits

snout is long and pointed

nostril is used for smelling, not breathing

pectoral fin lifts shark as it swims

◄ Sharks, rays and skates all belong to a class of fish called Chondrichthyes, the cartilaginous fishes. Sharks consist of around 375 species. Scientists group them into eight orders according to the physical characteristics that they share.

SHARK FAMILY TREE

no anal fin

flattened body
SQUATINIFORMES (angel sharks)

long snout
PRISTIOPHORIFORMES (sawsharks)

rounded body
(sleeper sharks
SQUALIFORMES and dogfish)
short snout

1 dorsal fin; 6–7 gill slits

HEXANCHIFORMES (cow sharks)

nictitating membranes (inner eyelids)
CARCHARHINIFORMES (ground sharks)

mouth behind eyes

anal fin

no spines on dorsal fin

LAMNIFORMES (mackerel sharks)
no nictitating membranes (inner eyelids)

ORECTOLOBIFORMES (carpet sharks)
mouth in front of eyes

2 dorsal fins; 5 gill slits

HETERODONTIFORMES (bullhead sharks)
spines on dorsal fin

On the move

All sharks swim by moving their heads from side to side. This movement passes down the body in waves, becoming more exaggerated as it reaches the caudal (tail) fin. The push of the tail against the water thrusts the shark forwards. At the same time, water flows over the pectoral and pelvic fins, which are shaped like aircraft wings – rounded at the front and sharp-edged at the back. This generates lift, and stops the shark from sinking. To move in different directions, the shark tilts its fins.

dorsal fin acts like a stabilizer and stops shark rolling

crescent-shaped caudal fin propels shark forwards

anal fin stabilizes shark as it swims

pelvic fin helps shark swim in a level position

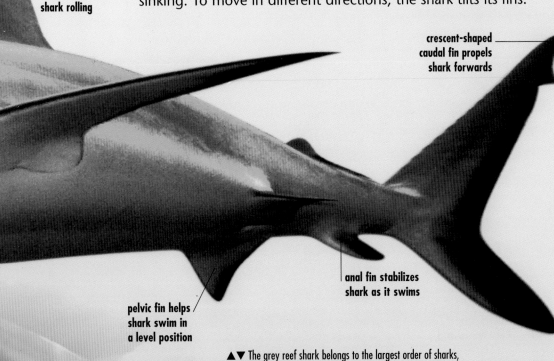

▲▼ The grey reef shark belongs to the largest order of sharks, the ground sharks. It is found in the Pacific and Indian oceans, often near coral reefs. Its white underside and grey back are a kind of camouflage known as countershading. Seen from above, the grey blends in with the dark water below. Seen from underneath, the white blends in with the sea's sunlit surface.

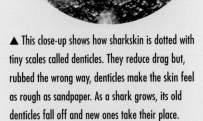

▲ This close-up shows how sharkskin is dotted with tiny scales called denticles. They reduce drag but, rubbed the wrong way, denticles make the skin feel as rough as sandpaper. As a shark grows, its old denticles fall off and new ones take their place.

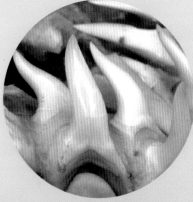

▲ These three rows of sawlike teeth belong to a great white. Sharks often lose teeth when killing and eating prey. As a tooth breaks off or wears out, another rotates forwards to take its place. Sharks can lose as many as 30,000 teeth in a lifetime.

▲ Like most sharks, this basking shark has five pairs of gill slits, or openings, on either side of its head. As the shark swims, water flows through its mouth, pushes across its gills and is then expelled through the gill slits. The gills filter oxygen from the water.

Inside a shark

Like all animals, a shark needs to breathe, move and eat. Its anatomy (body structure) has evolved to do all of these things efficiently. A shark 'breathes' through gills that take in oxygen from the water. It moves easily through the water because the cartilage that forms its skeleton is lighter than bone, and helps it to float. Its digestive system allows it to feed on sea creatures, such as other fish, shellfish or mammals, and to absorb the nutrients they contain.

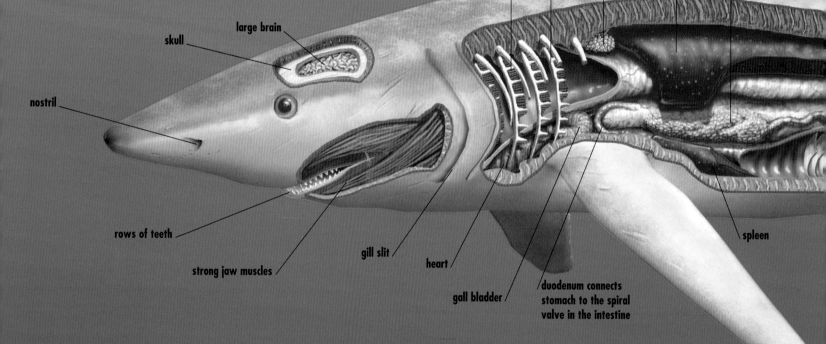

gill-raker like
tooth of a comb

pancreas aids
digestion

ovary and
eggs

gill arch

large liver
provides
buoyancy

large brain

skull

nostril

rows of teeth

strong jaw muscles

gill slit

heart

spleen

gall bladder

duodenum connects
stomach to the spiral
valve in the intestine

SHARK TAIL SHAPES

Great white sharks have crescent-shaped, symmetrical tail lobes. By controlling the speed at which the tail moves from side to side, they can switch from slow cruising to fast sprinting.

Tiger sharks have tails with a very long upper lobe and relatively short bottom lobe. Their asymmetric tails are good for twisting and turning, as well as for accelerating quickly when chasing prey.

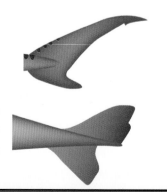

Nurse sharks are bottom-feeders that spend most of their time travelling eel-like along the seabed. They do not need to accelerate suddenly, so the bottom lobe has almost completely disappeared.

Cookiecutter sharks have tails with broad lobes that are nearly the same size. This shape is no good for fast swimming, but that does not matter. The lobes are bioluminescent, and lure prey towards the shark.

Energetic food processors

Sharks are successful hunters and determined feeders. They need to be, as they must eat up to 3 per cent of their body weight a day to survive. Their intestine is short and straight – a design that would normally let food pass through too quickly to be absorbed properly. However, sharks are also equipped with a valve – in a spiral, ring or scroll shape – that is lined with folds of membrane that slow digestion.

Staying afloat

Sharks do not have gas-filled swim bladders like bony fish, and most will sink if they stop swimming, but their very large liver helps to keep them buoyant. The liver has two large lobes (rounded parts) that store fats and an oil called squalene. This oil is what helps sharks to float, because it is lighter than water. The fats and squalene are also a store of energy. If the shark does not find enough to eat, it metabolizes them (chemically changes them into energy) to sustain itself until it finds food.

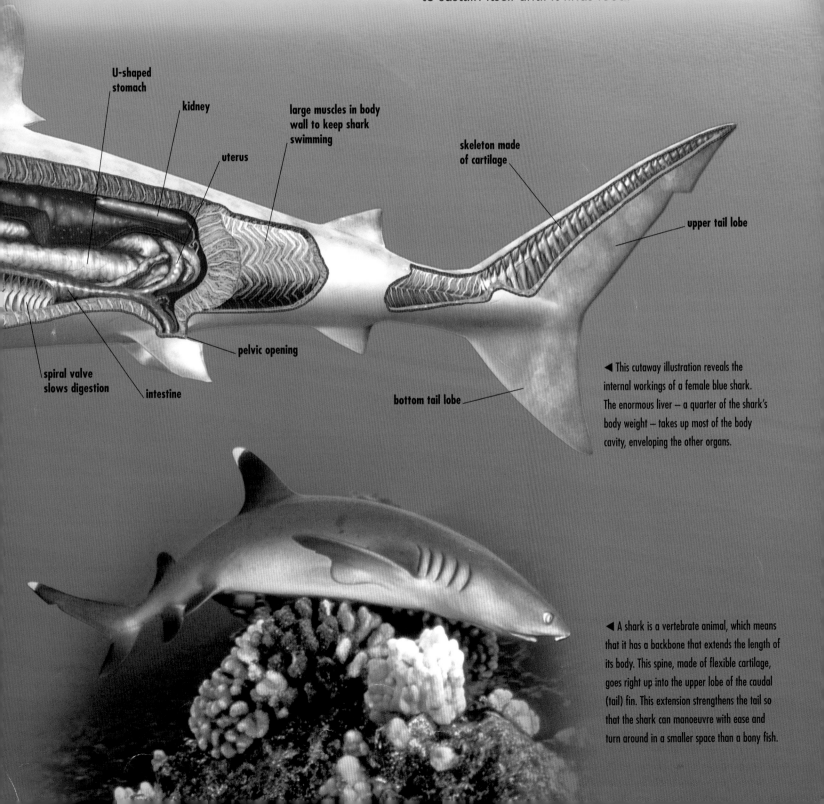

U-shaped stomach

kidney

large muscles in body wall to keep shark swimming

uterus

skeleton made of cartilage

upper tail lobe

pelvic opening

spiral valve slows digestion

intestine

bottom tail lobe

◀ This cutaway illustration reveals the internal workings of a female blue shark. The enormous liver – a quarter of the shark's body weight – takes up most of the body cavity, enveloping the other organs.

◀ A shark is a vertebrate animal, which means that it has a backbone that extends the length of its body. This spine, made of flexible cartilage, goes right up into the upper lobe of the caudal (tail) fin. This extension strengthens the tail so that the shark can manoeuvre with ease and turn around in a smaller space than a bony fish.

Giving birth

About a third of sharks – including wobbegongs, catsharks and horn sharks – are oviparous, which means that they reproduce by laying eggs. Like birds, bony fish and some reptiles, they lay fertilized eggs that are surrounded by a shell. The shells are soft while the eggs are in the uterus, but they harden in the water to form a protective case around the embryo. There are two other ways that sharks reproduce: giving birth to live young (viviparity) and producing eggs that hatch inside their body (ovoviviparity).

Viviparous sharks
Most of the sharks that give birth to live young are larger species, such as lemon, blue and hammerhead sharks. The embryos develop inside the uterus in a way similar to how human babies and other mammals grow. At first they feed on stored yolk. Later, they get oxygen and nutrients from their mother through a placenta, along an umbilical cord which also takes waste away. When they are fully developed, the shark pups are born live.

▼ A smallspotted catshark pup swims out of its egg case. Its mother laid the egg 6 to 12 months earlier, then swam away and left the pup to develop on its own. Egg cases often wash up on the beach and are nicknamed mermaids' purses.

Ovoviviparous sharks

Most sharks, including sand tigers, great whites and spiny dogfish, reproduce by ovoviviparity. The embryos develop in a shell-like case inside the uterus. When they are mature they hatch inside the female, which gives birth to live pups. The embryos are not connected by placenta to the mother; instead they feed on yolk stored in a yolk sac. In the case of the sand tiger, the first embryo to use up its yolk becomes a cannibal, eating up the remaining embryos and any unfertilized eggs.

▶ This newborn spiny dogfish developed ovoviviparously, as an egg inside its mother's uterus. It is still attached to its yolk sac. Spiny dogfish have the longest-known gestation period of any shark — about 22 months — and produce litters of up to 16 pups. At birth they measure around 25cm, almost a quarter of their adult length.

▼ A lemon shark's pregnancy lasts 10 to 12 months. When she is ready to give birth, the shark swims into sheltered, coastal waters. Her litter may contain up to 17 pups. Each pup rests for a moment on the seabed then swims away, breaking the umbilical cord. It will stay in its nursery grounds for the first few years of its life.

Ancient sharks

Most prehistoric sharks were very different from the sharks in the seas today, but they were still recognizably sharks. Few complete shark fossils have been found because cartilage does not survive well, but there is plenty of fossil evidence in the form of teeth, scales and fin spines. The earliest shark fossils are in rocks that are 400 million years old.

▲ One of the strangest of the early sharks was the 2m-long *Stethacanthus*, which swam in the seas more than 360 million years ago (mya). Its anvil-shaped dorsal fin looks rather like an open mouth and may have evolved to attract a mate or to frighten off predators.

Fossil evidence

In October 1666, a Danish physician called Nicolas Steno made a discovery that changed history. He was dissecting the head of a large shark, caught off the coast of Italy, when he realized he had seen the teeth somewhere else. For centuries, *glossopetrae* ('tongue stones') had been used in courts across Europe as magical amulets. Steno recognized that *glossopetrae* were not snakes' tongues, as people had thought, but fossilized sharks' teeth. His findings marked the birth of a new science, palaeontology.

▶ *Megalodon* ('big tooth'), a shark that lived from 25 to 5 mya, seizes its whale prey in its 15cm-long teeth. One of the most formidable predators ever to have swum in the seas, *Megalodon* measured up to 15m long — about twice the size of a great white.

The first 'modern' sharks

About 350 million years ago (mya), prehistoric sharks began to split into different groups which had different characteristics. The ancestors of modern sharks appeared around 200 mya at the beginning of the Jurassic period, when dinosaurs roamed the earth. Most of the shark groups that swim in the seas today – including bullhead, goblin, sand, nurse, cow and angel sharks – evolved during this period. Great whites appeared at least 65 mya.

▶ This photograph shows part of an extraordinary fossil – a spiral of teeth from the jaw of a shark called *Helicoprion* that lived 280 to 225 mya. The fossil contains at least 180 teeth, with the oldest teeth on the outside, pushed there by the most recently formed teeth at the centre of the spiral.

▼ These fossil shark teeth are embedded in rock that is 40 million years old. They belonged to a prehistoric member of the mackerel shark family, which includes today's salmon sharks and porbeagles.

Record breakers

The oceans' watery depths are home to an incredible variety of sharks, each with habits and abilities that have evolved to fit in with its particular habitat and lifestyle. The shark family includes the biggest fish in the ocean, the whale shark, as well as some of the fastest, makos and porbeagles. Shark lifespans vary enormously, too. Some species live for only 20 or 30 years but others, such as the spiny dogfish, may reach 100 years old.

▲ This pygmy shark is around half its adult size. Mature females grow to around 24cm long and males are even smaller at as little as 17cm. The pygmy shark feeds near the surface at night, but moves to a depth of around 1,600m during the day. Its underside glows as it swims.

Smallest of all

There are several contenders for the title of smallest shark. Most spined pygmy sharks are 20–25cm, but a mature male has been measured at only 15cm long. The dwarf dogfish is a mere 16–22cm, while the dwarf lanternshark, which glows in the dark depths of the deep ocean, reaches only about 20cm. One female pygmy ribbontail catshark was a tiny 18cm long.

Giant sharks

At 15m long, the whale shark is the largest fish on earth. Its cavernous mouth is 1.5m across – large enough for a car to be driven into it. The whale shark is a filter-feeder (see pages 42–43). It swims along with its mouth wide open, scooping up krill, squid and small fish such as sardines and anchovies. The 10m-long basking shark, also a filter-feeder, is the second-largest shark. Its vast jaw may be up to 1m wide.

▼ A whale shark cruises near the surface. It is as big as a humpback whale and weighs up to 15 tonnes – the same as three elephants. Its liver alone may weigh a tonne. Whale sharks also hold the record for having the most pups at a time – several hundred in one litter.

▲ The fastest shark is probably the shortfin mako. It cuts through the water at 50km/h and may top 75km/h in short bursts, while chasing fast-moving fish and squid. The mako can also leap 6m out of the water to make a quick getaway from an angler's line.

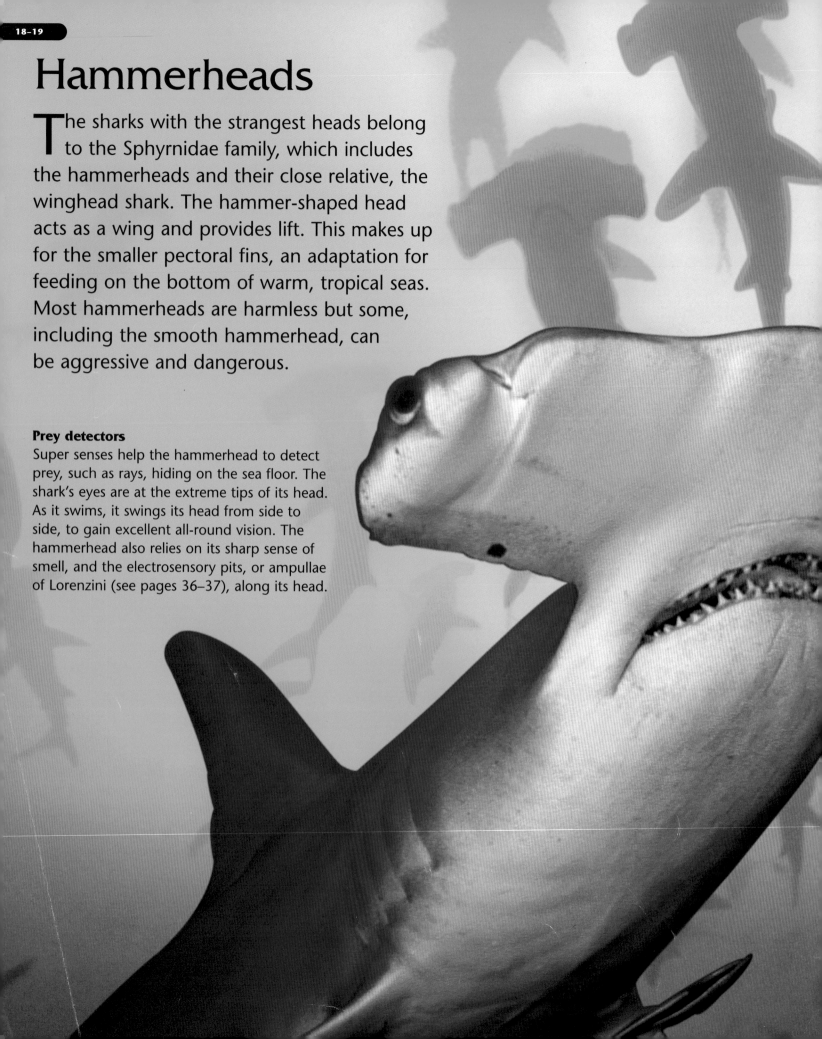

Hammerheads

The sharks with the strangest heads belong to the Sphyrnidae family, which includes the hammerheads and their close relative, the winghead shark. The hammer-shaped head acts as a wing and provides lift. This makes up for the smaller pectoral fins, an adaptation for feeding on the bottom of warm, tropical seas. Most hammerheads are harmless but some, including the smooth hammerhead, can be aggressive and dangerous.

Prey detectors

Super senses help the hammerhead to detect prey, such as rays, hiding on the sea floor. The shark's eyes are at the extreme tips of its head. As it swims, it swings its head from side to side, to gain excellent all-round vision. The hammerhead also relies on its sharp sense of smell, and the electrosensory pits, or ampullae of Lorenzini (see pages 36–37), along its head.

Schooling scalloped hammerheads

Scalloped hammerheads often gather in very large groups of up to 500 at a time. They are the only sharks to do this, coming together by day and breaking away to feed on their own at night. Most of the individuals are females, so perhaps they are gathering where males can find them easily, or to protect their young. Or the sharks may be seeking safety in numbers, like shoaling fish, to confuse predatory great whites, tiger sharks or killer whales.

◀ The distinctive hammer-shaped head of the scalloped hammerhead has a deep indentation at its centre. The hammer measures 60–90cm wide, which is roughly a quarter of the shark's body length.

◀ At 6m long, the great hammerhead is the largest member of the hammerhead family. It is also an aggressive hunter. It pins down stingrays with its head while biting off the wings.

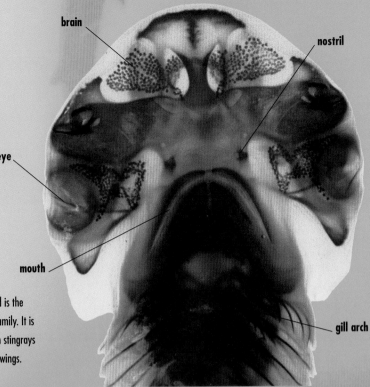

brain

nostril

eye

mouth

gill arch

▲ This transparent specimen of a bonnethead shark shows in blue the cartilage that forms the shape of its head, with its eyes at either end. The gill arches are beneath the jaws.

HEAD SHAPES

The great hammerhead is one of the world's largest predatory fish. Sometimes found in water only 1m deep, it uses its wide head to stir up sand on the seabed to find prey.

The scalloped hammerhead has four graceful lobes on the edge of its head. It is the most common hammerhead, often found close to shore in warm seas, bays and estuaries.

The bonnethead has a broad, spadelike head. It is the smallest hammerhead, about 1m long. Its main food is crustaceans, which it crushes with the large molars at the back of its jaw.

The winghead shark has the widest head in the family, relative to its size. Its body is about 1m long, but its head may be 50cm across. The large nostrils are nearly twice the width of the mouth.

Rarest of all

In January 1998, researchers reported sighting a rare Borneo river shark for the first time in a century. If sharks are described as 'rare' it usually means that they are seldom seen. The majority of species that are classified as rare live in the deep oceans, where they are unlikely to be spotted. Others, such as the whitetip soupfin and the great white, are rare because people have killed so many they have become endangered.

▼ The Greenland shark hunts in darkness under the Arctic ice, using its keen sense of smell to find food. Most Greenland sharks have been blinded by parasites called copepods, which attach themselves to the corneas in the sharks' eyes. The copepods glow in the gloom and may attract prey for the shark.

Deep-water monsters

One of the most extraordinary of the rarely seen deep-sea sharks is the megamouth, named for its enormous 1m-wide mouth. The first one was found off Hawaii in 1976; during the following 30 years only 38 were seen. The Greenland shark is another rare shark. It is found at depths of up to 550m in chilly Arctic waters, and only comes near the surface during winter months. A slow swimmer, it probably ambushes its fast-moving fish prey.

A living fossil

An extraordinary shark was first
identified off eastern Japan in 1898.
Japanese fishermen called it *tenguzame*, meaning
'goblin shark'. It is an example of a living fossil because it is
the only surviving member of a family that has been around for
100 million years – its teeth resemble those of the prehistoric
shark, *Scapanorhyncus*. The goblin shark lives on the sea floor
at depths of 350–1,200m. It feeds on squid and small fish.

▲ The goblin shark's long snout may contain
electrosensory canals (ampullae of Lorenzini) that help
the shark to detect prey. Once it has tracked down its
quarry, the shark's jaws shoot forwards to snap it up.

▼ Sawsharks and their relatives, sawfish, have suffered
greatly from habitat loss, overfishing and hunting for their
'saws', which have become collectors' items. This 7m-long
smalltooth sawfish is one of two species that live in US waters.
It uses its saw to wound and kill as it charges schools of fish,
and also to dig in the sediment for crabs and shellfish.

Near relatives

Rays, skates, guitarfish and sawfish look very different to sharks, but they are closely related. Like sharks, they have skeletons of cartilage instead of bone. They also have gill slits, although these are on the undersides of their bodies. Unlike sharks, they have flattened pectoral fins that stick out from their heads like wings.

Underwater fliers

There is no sight more graceful than the largest ray of all, the 7m-wide manta, gracefully flapping its pectoral fins. It looks like a strange bird in flight as it glides along. Rays and skates travel through the water in a completely different way from sharks. Torpedo rays send ripples along their bodies that propel them forwards. Leg skates have lobes (rounded pieces of skin) on their pelvic fins which they use to 'kick' themselves along.

▶ Spotted eagle rays swim in warm coastal waters, sometimes in large schools. They use their beak-like snouts to search in the mud for shellfish. Sometimes, when they are being hunted by predators such as silvertip and great hammerhead sharks, they can leap right out of the water.

▶ The common skate is a 3m-long predator, armed with up to 18 poisonous thorns along its tail. It feeds on crabs, lobsters and bottom-dwelling fish in deep European waters. Like many rays and skates, it is threatened by overfishing. Despite its name, the common skate is critically endangered.

Sting in the tail

Rays and skates use a variety of weapons. Many rays have poisonous spines on their whiplike tails, which can stun or kill prey and most predators (but not sharks). Electric rays may send an electrical current through the water of more than 200 volts – strong enough to stun the fish and crabs that they eat. The sawfish (see page 21) has a saw-shaped jaw for slashing at prey and defending itself against predators. Another distant relative, the chimaera, is armed with a venomous spine on its dorsal fin.

▼ A young snorkeller reaches out to touch a southern stingray in the Caribbean Sea. This stingray cruises over reefs, stopping to dig in the sandy patches for molluscs and crustaceans. It is also an ambush predator, lying camouflaged on the sandy seabed until it can surprise passing small fish or other prey.

Migration

Sharks sometimes travel long distances, but it is only recently that new technology, such as satellite tagging, has made it possible to track them. Some sharks migrate to mate and produce young in the best conditions. Others cross the oceans to find or follow food. Basking sharks also migrate vertically, moving between the surface and the ocean depths, depending on where plankton is most plentiful.

Incredible distances

Every year, female blue sharks feed and mate off the east coast of North America, and head 3,000km across the Atlantic to give birth off the coast of Africa. Tiger sharks also travel widely in the North Atlantic, sometimes reaching South America or Africa. Bull sharks have been found an amazing 4,200km up the Amazon river in the foothills of the Andes mountains in Peru.

North Atlantic Ocean

North America

blue shark

Pacific Ocean

tiger shark

Equator

bull shark

South America

South Atlantic Ocean

◄ Satellite tracking of tiger sharks has shown that they migrate to take advantage of different food sources. Some travel long distances to reach the coast of Hawaii each year when the albatross chicks fledge. Tiger sharks have also been tracked to Raine Island, off eastern Australia, during the turtle nesting season.

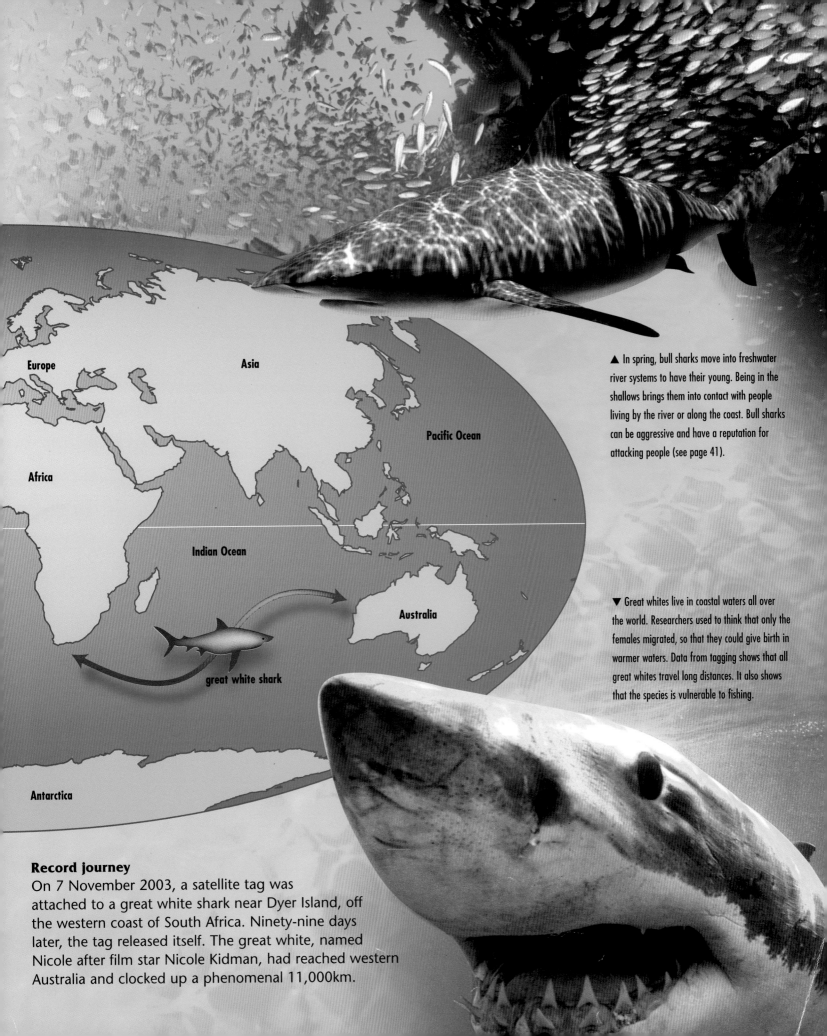

Europe

Asia

Africa

Pacific Ocean

Indian Ocean

Australia

great white shark

Antarctica

▲ In spring, bull sharks move into freshwater river systems to have their young. Being in the shallows brings them into contact with people living by the river or along the coast. Bull sharks can be aggressive and have a reputation for attacking people (see page 41).

▼ Great whites live in coastal waters all over the world. Researchers used to think that only the females migrated, so that they could give birth in warmer waters. Data from tagging shows that all great whites travel long distances. It also shows that the species is vulnerable to fishing.

Record journey
On 7 November 2003, a satellite tag was attached to a great white shark near Dyer Island, off the western coast of South Africa. Ninety-nine days later, the tag released itself. The great white, named Nicole after film star Nicole Kidman, had reached western Australia and clocked up a phenomenal 11,000km.

Open ocean

The ocean expanses are home to many different pelagic (open-water) sharks. The larger sharks cruise along near or at the surface. There are vast distances to cover and, in open water, they need speed to catch fast-moving fish prey such as tuna, mackerel and marlin. On occasions, both the great white and the shortfin mako have been known to breach, or leap out of the water, while hunting.

Hunting the seas

To be an efficient open-ocean hunter, a shark must be either large and powerful or exceptionally streamlined. Large oceanic sharks include the oceanic whitetip, silky, blue and thresher sharks. They spend most of their time cruising slowly at the surface, but are capable of a rapid burst of speed in pursuit of prey. The most streamlined oceanic sharks include the torpedo-shaped porbeagle and salmon sharks, as well as the shortfin mako, which is the fastest shark of all.

▲ Blue sharks, found in tropical and temperate seas worldwide, are the most common of the large pelagic sharks. They measure about 3.5m long and are easily recognized by their deep blue back and sides. These ones are hunting anchovies in the Pacific Ocean.

◄ At 3m long, the pelagic thresher is the smallest and least-known of the three species of thresher that live in the open ocean. Its scythelike tail — an extended caudal fin — is about the same length as its body. The shark may use it as a weapon to slash or stun fish, or possibly even to herd them.

Supercharged predators

Most sharks are ectothermic (cold-blooded), which means that they take on the temperature of their surroundings. However, some of the faster-moving oceanic sharks are partly endothermic (warm-blooded), which means that they are able to raise their body temperature. The common thresher can maintain a body temperature as much as 13°C higher than the surrounding water. Scientists believe that, by warming parts of their bodies such as their flanks, these sharks are able to beat their tails more – and pursue their prey more quickly.

▶ Oceanic whitetip sharks are fierce, solitary predators. They live in open water, usually at depths of around 150m, and are only occasionally seen near land. They eat a wide variety of food, including turtles, seabirds and tuna (which they catch by swimming through tuna schools with their mouths open).

Deep-sea hunters

Sharks are successful even in the cold, dark depths of the ocean. Some, such as the Greenland shark, are slow-moving and cold-blooded, having the same temperature as the very cold water in which they swim. Others, such as the Galápagos shark, are fast-moving visitors to these dark regions. A few make their own eerie light, to lure prey in the gloom.

Down in the depths

Sharks that live deep below the surface are usually small. They often have blunt noses that they use to forage for food, and tails that are flat or have large upper lobes. They swim sluggishly because the cold slows their metabolism (how their body makes energy from food). And they usually give birth to only two or three young at a time.

▲ *Alvin* was the first deep-sea submersible to be able to carry passengers. It has been in operation since 1964. It can dive to a maximum depth of 4,500m and has allowed scientists to observe deep-sea sharks in their habitat.

Gonatus squid

cookiecutter shark

great lanternshark

▲ The cookiecutter shark, found at depths of 85–3,500m, has a cigar-shaped body up to 50cm long. Around its middle it has a network of photophores – round, light-producing organs that give off a greenish light. Their glow brings curious prey within reach of the shark's wickedly sharp teeth.

▲ The great lanternshark has been found at depths of 4,500m. In deeper waters, more females of this shark are found than males. The sharks, up to 65cm long, also get smaller as the depth increases. Lanternsharks are named for their light-producing photophores, which attract prey such as deep-sea squid and crustaceans.

▼ The eel-like frilled shark is about 2m long. It is named for the frilly edges of its six gills, and it is the only shark to have a gill (the one nearest its mouth) that wraps right under its throat. With a mouth packed with broad, multi-pointed teeth, the frilled shark feeds on small, deep-sea bony fish and squid.

frilled shark

bluntnose shark

▼ Found as deep as 3,700m, the Portuguese dogfish has long, daggerlike teeth in its upper jaw, and shorter, slanted teeth in its lower jaw. Like the cookiecutter, it takes circular bites out of live prey (see page 35), such as dolphins, whales, seals and fish, including other sharks.

Portuguese dogfish

▲ The well-named bluntnose shark is 130cm long and has six gills. It usually lives in depths of at least 90m and has been found at 1,875m. This shark is a vertical migrator, travelling towards the surface at night to feed, and returning to the depths before dawn. Unusually for a deep-sea shark, it gives birth to very large litters of between 20 and 110 pups.

Sensory tools

Sharks need an acute sense of smell to find food in the murky ocean depths. They also use their ampullae of Lorenzini to pick up tiny electrical signals from their prey. Some sharks, such as the green lanternshark, have extra-large eyes to make up for the poor visibility in the gloom. A few deep-sea sharks have bodies that light up so they can distract predators or attract prey.

On the reef

The clear waters surrounding coral reefs are home to many kinds of shark. In the Bahamas, lemon sharks give birth in shallow bays surrounded by mangroves. Galápagos sharks swim in schools off tropical islands around the world, and sandtiger sharks hover above the bottom of rocky reefs off South Africa. Reefs provide a rich habitat because they shelter turtles, fish, anemones, crustaceans and molluscs for sharks to hunt.

► With its downturned mouth and the ridges above its eyes, the whitetip reef shark can appear to be frowning. It is named for the distinctive tips on its dorsal and upper caudal fins. It locates prey such as octopuses and crabs by sound and vibration, traps them in rocky crevices, then wriggles its slender body in after them.

▼ The epaulette carpet shark is easily identified by the ocellus (a large, black eye-like spot) just above each pectoral fin. It is a bottom-dweller that uses its pectoral fins to 'walk' or even 'run' along the seabed. Just over 1m long, it hunts at night for crabs, shrimps and small fish hiding among the coral.

Balancing act

The three most common sharks on Indo-Pacific coral reefs are the whitetip reef, blacktip reef and grey reef sharks. Although they are interested in similar prey, they do not have to compete with one another. They either hunt at different times of day or at the same time but at different depths. The whitetip reef shark is a night hunter that seeks out prey in waters 10–40m deep. The other two species both hunt at dawn and dusk. However, the blacktip pursues prey in lagoons close to the shore, while the grey reef feeds further out in clearer waters up to 100m deep.

The world's largest reef

At least 120 species of sharks and rays may be found at the Great Barrier Reef off northern Australia. They range from the epaulette carpet shark that never moves off the reef to migratory species such as the whale shark. Some of the sharks, including whitetip reef sharks, have thick skin to protect against the sharp coral. The colourful fish and shellfish attract bottom-feeders such as angel sharks and zebra bullheads, as well as fast hunters such as the tiger shark. Sometimes the tables are turned, when large coral grouper fish prey upon the smaller reef sharks.

▶ Grey reef sharks are active and social sharks that patrol the reef for squid and fish, sometimes in large schools of up to 100 individuals. They measure around 1.6m long and are prey to larger sharks, including the silvertip shark.

▼ With its spotted body, the zebra shark appears at first glance to have been given the wrong name, but it is so-called for its stripy, brown-and-cream young. Like many species that swim in bright, shallow waters, zebra sharks have tiny eyes. They hunt at night for molluscs, small fish and even sea snakes.

SUMMARY OF CHAPTER 1: MEET THE SHARK

Rulers of the seas

The world of the shark is a complex one. The 375 species in the family are very varied in appearance and lifestyle. However, what they do have in common – their physical characteristics and their ability as predatory hunters – has helped them to survive successfully for millions of years. During all that time, they have maintained their position as top predators in the marine food chain.

Classifying the shark

All biologists classify living things according to the system devised by Carl von Linné, known as Linnaeus. He was a Swedish naturalist who published his *Systema Naturae* in 1758. Under his system, which was based on observing external characteristics, shark classification is relatively straightforward. Today, however, the classification system is being modified all the time as more and more is discovered about particular species of shark.

A variety of habitats

Sharks live in pelagic (open-ocean) and benthic (bottom-dwelling) habitats worldwide. The pelagic sharks are sleek and streamlined, and clearly designed for speed. They include the fastest sharks such as the mako, with its sprint speed of more than 20 body-lengths per second. Benthic sharks look very different – most have blunt noses, and many have flat bodies. They swim slowly and often ambush, rather than chase, their prey. Some, such as the angel shark, are very well camouflaged.

The puffadder shyshark is hard to spot in its reef habitat off the coast of South Africa.

Go further...

Find out about the biology of sharks and rays:
www.elasmo-research.org

Discover exactly how sharks work:
science.howstuffworks.com/shark6

Investigate this great site that covers all aspects of sharks and rays:
http://www.seaworld.org
/animal-info/info-books/sharks-&-rays/

The Florida Museum of Natural History website recommends books and advises on how to avoid a shark attack: www.flmnh.ufl.edu/
fish/Kids/kids.htm

Eyewitness: Shark by Miranda MacQuitty (Dorling Kindersley, 2002)

Ichthyologist
A zoologist who specializes in fish.

Naturalist
A person who studies or is an expert in natural history.

Palaeontologist
A scientist who studies the forms of life that existed in prehistoric times.

Scientist
An expert in at least one area of science who uses scientific method to do research.

Zoologist
A scientist who studies animals and their characteristics, and classifies them.

See shark exhibits at: The Natural History Museum, Cromwell Road, London SW7 5BD, UK
Telephone: +44 (0)20 7942 5000
www.nhm.ac.uk

Discover wonderful shark species at:
Australian Museum, 6 College Street, Sydney, NSW 2010, Australia
Telephone: +61 (2) 9320 6000
www.austmus.gov.au

Attend shark week each August at:
The Aquarium of Niagara,
701 Whirlpool Street, Niagara Falls, NY 14301, USA
Telephone: +1 (800) 500 4609
www.aquariumofniagara.org

CHAPTER 2

Shark attack!

Although they are the fiercest of predators, sharks do not naturally feed on humans. Fewer than a dozen of the 375 species of shark are really considered dangerous to people – and their attacks may be cases of mistaken identity. Sharks could confuse the shape of a human, particularly on a surfboard, with a seal or sea lion. In other instances, they may be provoked by boats too near to their food source or pups. Sharks are the ocean's top predators, and most have no need to fear attack from other hunters. Only a few smaller ones are attacked – by other sharks or by killer whales. When the fiercest shark of all, the great white, hunts, it may kill its prey with a burst of speed that throws the animal right out of the water. It probably does this to stun the animal and avoid being injured by claws or teeth.

A great white breaches with a Cape fur seal in its jaws.

Teeth

Sharks' jaws carry an incredible conveyor belt of teeth that are superbly designed to catch and eat prey. Every time a tooth or row of teeth falls out, the conveyor belt carries new teeth forwards. The process continues endlessly until the animal dies. Some of the biggest sharks, such as the whale shark, have the smallest teeth. Instead of chewing their food, they filter it using their gill-rakers (see pages 42–43).

▶ A grey nurse shark goes in for the kill. Its lower jaw has dropped down and the upper jaw has moved forwards to expose the top teeth. Moments before it makes contact, nictitating membranes (inner eyelids) close to protect its eyes against scratches from the struggling prey.

◀ A scientist who specializes in fossil reconstruction stands inside a lifesize model of the prehistoric shark *Megalodon*'s jaws, which are estimated to have been 2.1m tall and 1.8m wide. He is holding the actual jaws of a large great white shark. *Megalodon*'s jaw size is estimated from the size of fossil teeth.

Teeth through the ages

Like sharks themselves, sharks' teeth have become smaller since prehistoric times. However, their effectiveness has not diminished. The extinct giant shark *Megalodon* (see page 14), which hunted enormous whales, had serrated teeth that were up to 15cm long – the size of a person's hand. Its modern relative, the great white, may be half the size but it is also the top predator in its habitat. It uses its 7.5cm-long teeth to bite and weaken its prey.

▼ The cookiecutter shark got its name because it takes cookie-shaped bites out of larger marine animals such as dolphins and whales. It attaches its lips to its victim by suction, then spins its eel-like body. The small, upright teeth in its upper jaw and the large, triangular teeth in its lower jaw cut out a plug of flesh.

Teeth for every occasion

The slender, spearlike teeth in the jaws of grey nurse, lemon and shortfin mako sharks are used to catch slippery fish and squid. Bullhead, nurse and smoothhound sharks are equipped with blunt, crushing teeth for tackling the tough shells of molluscs or crustaceans. The fearsome great white and tiger sharks have triangular cutting teeth, just right for taking chunks out of seals and other large prey.

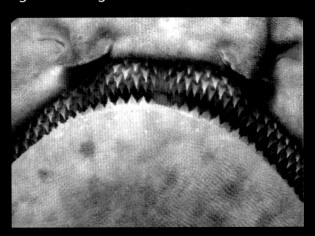

▲ The swellshark is a nocturnal hunter that lives in kelp forests in the eastern Pacific Ocean, from California to central Chile. It is 1m long and has a large mouth filled with rows of tiny, pointed teeth. They are very sharp and used to grasp hold of the fish and crustaceans that the swellshark catches on or near the sea floor.

Targeting prey

Sharks have five senses just like humans – sight, hearing, feeling, smell and taste. They also use pressure sensors along their bodies to detect the movement of prey as far as 10m away. And sharks have another remarkable sense – electrosensory perception. This allows them to detect the weak electrical field generated by all marine animals.

▼ The Caribbean reef shark patrols coral reefs from Florida to Brazil, but it is particularly common in the Caribbean Sea. Its main prey is large fish such as tuna. The Caribbean reef shark is particularly sensitive to the very low-frequency sounds that travel through water, and this enables it to target moving fish easily.

▲ Sharks have a network of sensory cells along the sides of the body and head. This network is called the lateral line. The cells detect vibrations in the water, especially low-frequency sound waves, such as those produced by a wounded fish.

Sniffing things out

Sharks use their sense of smell not only to locate prey, but also to find a mate and to navigate. Behind the flaps of skin that form the nostrils are nasal sacs lined with sensitive cells. These pick up odours from the water that continuously flows through the nostrils. When a shark detects a smell, it turns into the current and heads straight for the source.

▼ The pyjama shark, or striped catshark, has feelers on its nose called barbels. The shark uses the barbels to taste and feel its way to its crustacean and fish prey. Some sharks, such as nurse and angel sharks, have longer barbels that they use to probe the sand for food.

Specially sensitive

There are two different kinds of sensory perception in a shark. The lateral line, which runs the length of the shark's body, responds to pressure changes and movement in the water, and is effective at a distance. The ampullae of Lorenzini are jelly-filled pits spread around the shark's head in clusters. Each pit houses a sensor that detects electrical signals from the muscle movements of prey when the shark is closing in on it.

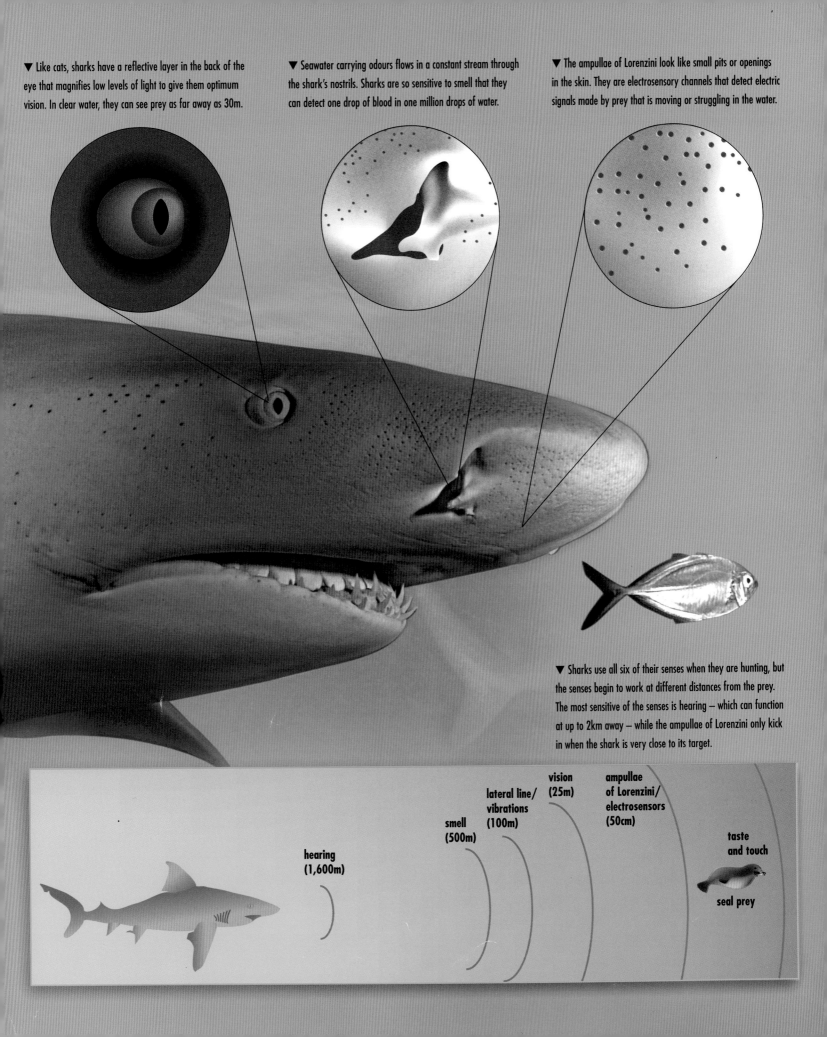

▼ Like cats, sharks have a reflective layer in the back of the eye that magnifies low levels of light to give them optimum vision. In clear water, they can see prey as far away as 30m.

▼ Seawater carrying odours flows in a constant stream through the shark's nostrils. Sharks are so sensitive to smell that they can detect one drop of blood in one million drops of water.

▼ The ampullae of Lorenzini look like small pits or openings in the skin. They are electrosensory channels that detect electric signals made by prey that is moving or struggling in the water.

▼ Sharks use all six of their senses when they are hunting, but the senses begin to work at different distances from the prey. The most sensitive of the senses is hearing — which can function at up to 2km away — while the ampullae of Lorenzini only kick in when the shark is very close to its target.

vision
(25m)

ampullae
of Lorenzini/
electrosensors
(50cm)

lateral line/
vibrations
(100m)

smell
(500m)

taste
and touch

hearing
(1,600m)

seal prey

Hunting in packs

Not all sharks are lone killers. Blue sharks are one of many species that feed in groups, while grey nurse and copper sharks co-operate to hunt prey. These sharks have developed such techniques because they allow them to catch more food than they could by hunting on their own.

▶ These copper sharks in the Indian Ocean have created a huge baitball of sardines. As they charge through the baitball, they snatch big mouthfuls of the fish. Sometimes, dolphins join sharks to prey on large baitballs like this one.

No escape

Herding prey so that it cannot escape is an efficient way of hunting. Groups of grey nurse sharks encourage bluefish to swim into shallow waters by whipping their tails – an action that generates underwater waves. Several shark species practise baitballing, a technique that involves circling a school of fish so that they swim together for protection and become an easy target. Copper and silky sharks both hunt in this way.

▶ Eyes are essential for seeing and closing in on prey (see pages 36–37), but they can be damaged at the moment of attack. This tiger shark's eye is protected by a nictitating membrane (inner eyelid) that draws across the eye just before feeding.

▼ This feeding frenzy of grey reef sharks was photographed on the Great Barrier Reef, off the coast of Australia. The shark at the top is so carried away that it has forgotten its primary target and clamped its jaws firmly on to one of the other sharks.

In a frenzy

When a group of sharks finds a lot of prey animals, the blood in the water and the unusual movements of the frightened fish can excite and confuse the sharks. They circle and lunge – even at each other. The activity attracts more sharks and the frenzy grows. Even solitary sharks, such as the oceanic whitetip, take part in feeding frenzies.

Man-eaters

According to the International Shark Attack File, which reports on shark attacks worldwide, three sharks pose the greatest threat to people: the great white, tiger and bull sharks. However, the total number of shark attack victims is fewer than 100 per year, of which only 5 to 15 are fatal. A person is 250 times more likely to be killed by lightning than by a shark.

▼ The great white often attacks by rising at a steep angle from below. It takes a bite then releases its prey, wounded but alive. The shark circles and waits for the prey to weaken from blood loss before returning to kill and feed. This bite-spit-wait technique is very effective.

▲ Although there are very few shark attacks, they are still horrific. Beaches carry warning signs in areas where they are likely to happen. This sign alerts swimmers, surfers and divers to danger from some of the 40 species of shark in Hawaiian waters.

Most feared

The great white has the worst reputation of the man-eaters, and carries out more fatal attacks a year than any other shark. With triangular, razor-sharp teeth up to 7.5cm long and the ability to smell a drop of blood in 100 litres of water, it is a truly frightening predator. It is difficult to be exact about shark attack statistics because it is not always certain which species of shark carried out an attack. However, the International Shark Attack File estimates that there have been only 430 attacks by great whites since 1580.

Other killers

The tiger shark is an aggressive, large shark that swims in tropical seas. It is 3m long and a voracious hunter. Its diet is very varied, and it is notorious for its attacks on divers and surfers. The bull shark is also much feared. It is a marine shark but it can tolerate fresh water and often travels up rivers. It has been responsible for many attacks on bathers and swimmers in the Ganges, Zambezi and Amazon rivers.

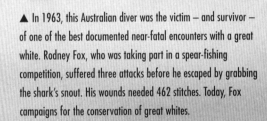

▲ In 1963, this Australian diver was the victim – and survivor – of one of the best documented near-fatal encounters with a great white. Rodney Fox, who was taking part in a spear-fishing competition, suffered three attacks before he escaped by grabbing the shark's snout. His wounds needed 462 stitches. Today, Fox campaigns for the conservation of great whites.

Giant filter-feeders

The filter-feeders of the shark world are enormous. This is because they often travel a long way to find the zooplankton on which they feed – whale sharks will follow plankton blooms all over the eastern Indian Ocean. Filter-feeders need a large storage capacity and a large mouth so that when they do find food, they can process great quantities of it.

► This sample of zooplankton, photographed under a microscope, is from the Great Barrier Reef, Australia. It includes the larvae of sea cucumbers, copepods (small crustaceans) and crabs. Zooplankton is seasonal – more food is available during the spring and summer months than in winter.

▼ The 10m-long basking shark cruises along near the surface at 4km/h with its cavernous jaws stretched wide, revealing its white gill arches and the bristly, black gill-rakers in-between. At regular intervals, the shark closes its mouth, flutters its gills and swallows the plankton that it has collected.

Ways of feeding

Only three living sharks are filter-feeders: the whale shark, basking shark and megamouth. These sharks all forage in the same way. They swim forwards with open mouths, passively scooping up anything in their path. At regular intervals, they close their mouths, water is pushed out through the gills, and prey filtered through the gill-rakers is swallowed. This is filter-feeding. The whale shark and megamouth also suction-feed, actively sucking in prey.

Deepwater monster

The megamouth is more than 5m long, and named for its gigantic, 1m-wide mouth. It has up to 100 rows of tiny teeth in each jaw and an enormous tongue. It also has bioluminescent spots called photophores around its mouth that may attract plankton and small fish.

► Whale sharks are often attended by remoras, 1m-long fish with suckers on their heads that they use to fix themselves to their host's belly. The remoras gain a free ride, protection from predators and a good place from which to ambush prey. They can also eat any scraps of food that fall from the shark's mouth.

megamouth filter-feeding with mouth open

megamouth suction-feeding with jaw extended

▲ When the megamouth suction-feeds, it juts out its upper jaw and widens its throat. By doing this it creates a suction that pulls in seawater filled with zooplankton. Then it closes its mouth, and the food is filtered in the usual way by the gill-rakers.

Bottom-feeders

The ocean floor is rich in pickings for sharks adapted to living there. Benthic sharks are bottom-feeders that live on or near the seabed. Some have flattened bodies, and markings or colours that help them to hide from passing prey or larger predators. Some crawl along the bottom on their fins, searching for prey in sand, mud or seaweed. Others glide around reefs and rocky areas, sucking out food from rocks and crevices.

▼ The tasselled wobbegong lives in the warm seas of the western Pacific. It is well camouflaged against the rocks and coral reefs. Its shaggy beard of tentacles looks like seaweed, and attracts prey including flatfish, squid, cuttlefish and crabs.

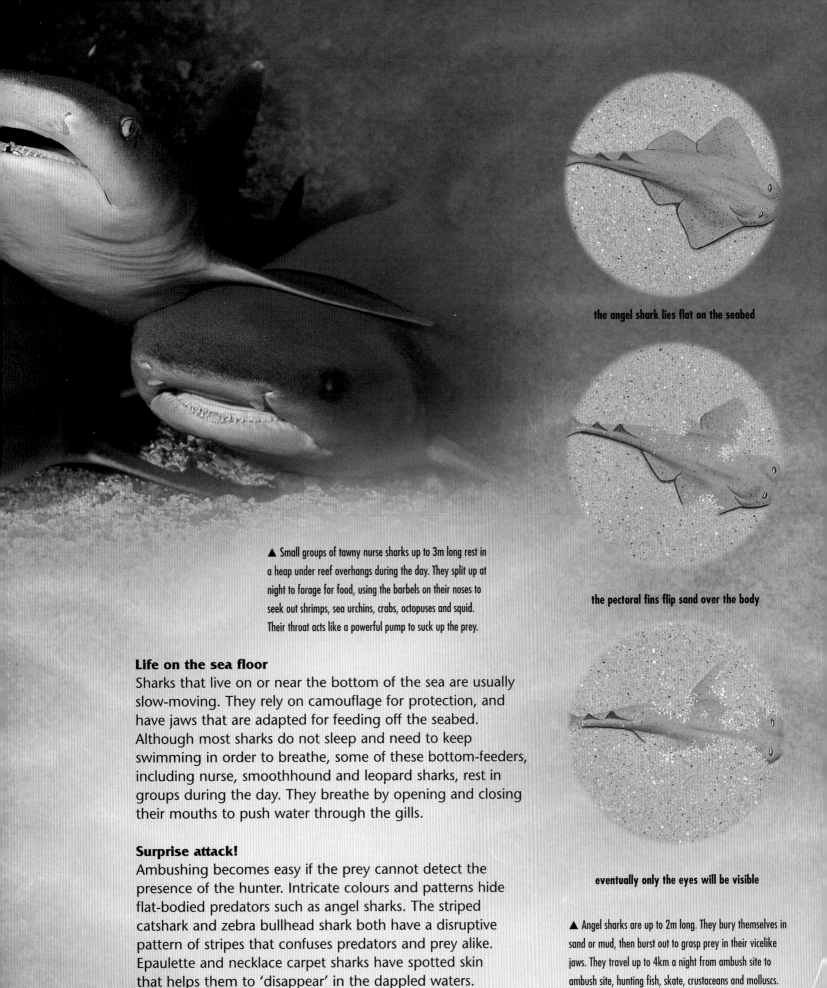

the angel shark lies flat on the seabed

the pectoral fins flip sand over the body

eventually only the eyes will be visible

▲ Small groups of tawny nurse sharks up to 3m long rest in a heap under reef overhangs during the day. They split up at night to forage for food, using the barbels on their noses to seek out shrimps, sea urchins, crabs, octopuses and squid. Their throat acts like a powerful pump to suck up the prey.

Life on the sea floor

Sharks that live on or near the bottom of the sea are usually slow-moving. They rely on camouflage for protection, and have jaws that are adapted for feeding off the seabed. Although most sharks do not sleep and need to keep swimming in order to breathe, some of these bottom-feeders, including nurse, smoothhound and leopard sharks, rest in groups during the day. They breathe by opening and closing their mouths to push water through the gills.

Surprise attack!

Ambushing becomes easy if the prey cannot detect the presence of the hunter. Intricate colours and patterns hide flat-bodied predators such as angel sharks. The striped catshark and zebra bullhead shark both have a disruptive pattern of stripes that confuses predators and prey alike. Epaulette and necklace carpet sharks have spotted skin that helps them to 'disappear' in the dappled waters.

▲ Angel sharks are up to 2m long. They bury themselves in sand or mud, then burst out to grasp prey in their vicelike jaws. They travel up to 4km a night from ambush site to ambush site, hunting fish, skate, crustaceans and molluscs.

SUMMARY OF CHAPTER 2: SHARK ATTACK!

Perfect predators

Sharks are superb at hunting, and they are also efficient killers. Most sharks use sharp teeth to despatch their prey, but the largest ones, such as the whale and basking sharks, are filter-feeders. Some sharks hunt co-operatively, working together in groups or herding fish with their tails. All animals use their senses to target prey, but sharks' senses are particularly acute. Sharks have the added advantages of being able to detect the movement of prey using their lateral line system, and the electric field around prey using their electrosensory ampullae of Lorenzini.

The truth about sharks

Sharks are not bloodthirsty killers: they hunt to survive. By preying upon animals lower down the food chain, sharks help to keep the oceans' ecosystems in balance. The reality about shark attacks on people is that there are very few per year – only about 50 to 70 worldwide, of which between 5 and 15 are fatal. It is difficult to give accurate shark attack statistics because eyewitnesses may have trouble identifying the species, while some attacks are simply not witnessed or reported.

The ISAF

The International Shark Attack File (ISAF) is an organization that compiles the world's most accurate list of shark attacks. It is managed by the American Elasmobranch Society and the Florida Museum of Natural History. The information collected for the ISAF dates as far back as the mid-1500s, and the data has been submitted and investigated by scientists all over the world.

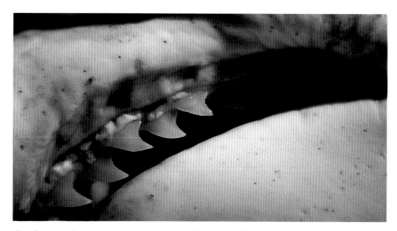

This close-up shows the curved teeth of a blue shark. The hooked shape and serrated edges enable the shark to hold slippery squid and fish.

Go further...

Shark attacks through the ages and throughout the world are detailed here: www.shark-info.com/shark-history

For up-to-the-minute statistics on shark attacks worldwide, visit: www.sharkattackfile.net

To learn how to avoid a shark attack, consult the International Shark Attack File on: http://www.flmnh.ufl.edu/fish/kids/Avoid/avoid.htm

The Encyclopedia of Sharks by Steve and Jane Parker (Firefly Books, 2002)

The Truth About Great White Sharks by Mary Cerullo and Jeffrey Rotman (Chronicle Books, 2007)

Diver
A person who dives or works underwater, often using breathing apparatus and weighted clothing.

Microbiologist
A biologist who specializes in micro-organisms and their structure.

Oceanographer
A scientist who explores and studies all aspects of the oceans, including their physical geography and the animals and plants that live in them.

Statistician
A mathematician who gathers together data and compares it.

The San Diego Natural History Museum has an online Shark School, or you can visit in person for information on various sharks, including ten local species: 1788 El Prado, San Diego, CA 92101, USA Telephone: +1 (619) 232 3821 www.sdnhm.org

The London Aquarium houses more than 350 marine species, including sandtiger, nurse, brown, dogfish and zebra sharks and stingrays: County Hall, Westminster Bridge Road, London SE1 7PB, UK Telephone: +44 (0) 20 7967 8000 www.londonaquarium.co.uk

CHAPTER 3

Sharks and people

It is slowly dawning on people that sharks do not pose as great a threat as they had feared, but there is still a long way to go. By 2017, an estimated 20 species of living sharks will have become extinct. Sharks are still ruthlessly hunted for food, trophies, skins and traditional medicines. Thousands more are trapped each year in nets, either intended to catch other fish or set up to keep sharks away from beaches. Pollution poisons the whole food chain and threatens shark nurseries. Many species grow slowly, mate late and produce relatively few offspring. These species are in real danger of being killed before they have had a chance to reproduce. Sharks help to keep populations of prey animals in check. By fishing too many sharks or putting them in danger in other ways, people put whole ecosystems at risk. It is essential that all countries help to monitor and preserve shark populations.

From the safety of a shark cage, divers watch Galápagos sharks off the coast of Hawaii.

Myths and legends

Sharks are sea monsters in mythology; gods or demons in traditional cultures; and the subject of paintings, sculptures and stories all over the world. Shark legends have been around since prehistoric times, but the first written accounts of sharks are from the ancient Greeks, who believed sharks to be a source of magical powers.

Around the world

Mythical sharks appear in many guises. In Japan, the storm god Samehito is known as the 'shark man', while the Hawaiians had a shark god called Moho. Some peoples build myths around the actions of sharks. The Warao Indians of the Orinoco river basin in South America tell of Nohi-Abassi, a man who trained a shark to kill his mother-in-law but was in his turn killed, his leg becoming the constellation Orion. In the South Pacific, people on the Solomon Islands believed that sharks were their ancestors and offered them human sacrifices.

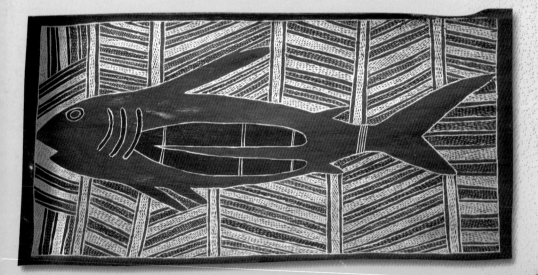

▲ In the art of the aboriginal people of Australia, the shark represents an ancestor spirit. This bark painting of a tiger shark is part of the X-ray tradition, a 4,000-year-old painting style that shows an animal's internal organs and bone structure.

▶ Jonah disappears into the mouth of a big fish in an illustration from a Hebrew manuscript of 1299. The 16th-century French naturalist Guillaume Rondelet suggested that the Biblical story was wrong and that Jonah was swallowed by a shark, not a whale.

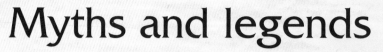

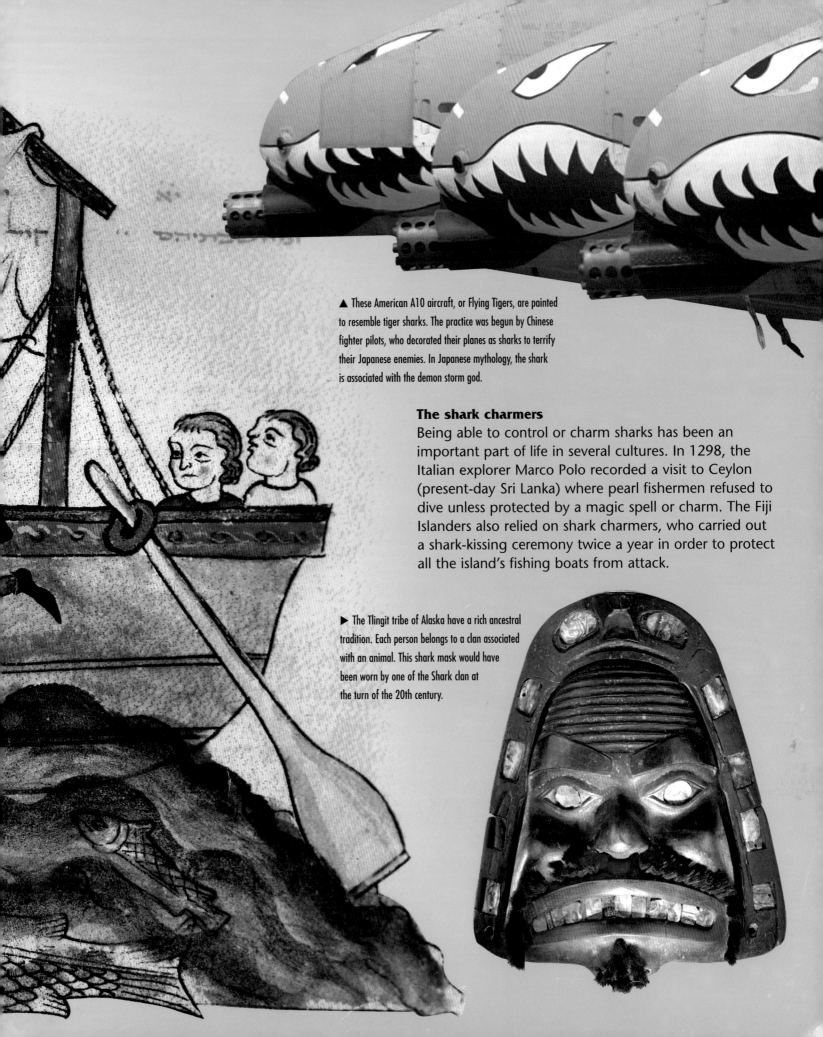

▲ These American A10 aircraft, or Flying Tigers, are painted to resemble tiger sharks. The practice was begun by Chinese fighter pilots, who decorated their planes as sharks to terrify their Japanese enemies. In Japanese mythology, the shark is associated with the demon storm god.

The shark charmers

Being able to control or charm sharks has been an important part of life in several cultures. In 1298, the Italian explorer Marco Polo recorded a visit to Ceylon (present-day Sri Lanka) where pearl fishermen refused to dive unless protected by a magic spell or charm. The Fiji Islanders also relied on shark charmers, who carried out a shark-kissing ceremony twice a year in order to protect all the island's fishing boats from attack.

▶ The Tlingit tribe of Alaska have a rich ancestral tradition. Each person belongs to a clan associated with an animal. This shark mask would have been worn by one of the Shark clan at the turn of the 20th century.

Shark tales

Over the centuries, sharks have made their appearance in art and sculpture, and in more recent times played their part in novels and films. But it is the man-eaters – the great white and the tiger shark – that obsess people, and the fear of those teeth that is exploited by artists, writers and movie directors.

Anchor, a winghead hammerhead shark

Chum, a mako shark

Dory, a blue tang fish

Marlin, a clownfish

Sharks in fiction

Most sharks in literature appear during shipwrecks or epic sea battles. In *Moby Dick* (1851), sharks in a feeding frenzy attack the dead sperm whale that Captain Ahab is towing to land. Ernest Hemingway's *The Old Man and the Sea* (1952) tells of mako sharks devouring the marlin fish that the Old Man has battled so long to catch.

▲ *Watson and the Shark* (1776) by John Singleton Copley depicts the true story of Brook Watson, a 14-year-old sailor who was attacked by a shark while swimming. Amazingly, Watson survived, although he lost part of his right leg. He went on to become a rich merchant and, eventually, Lord Mayor of London.

Sharks at the movies

Jaws (1975) was not the first shark film, but it had a huge impact. It spawned a host of shark horror films, including three more *Jaws* movies, *Deep Blue Sea* (1999), *Open Water* (2004) and the *Shark Attack* films. It also inspired animations such as *Finding Nemo* (2003) and *A Shark's Tale* (2004).

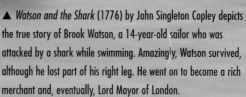

Bruce, a great white shark

JAWS

▲ Steven Spielberg's *Jaws* transformed the way people thought about the great white shark. From then on, no one could hear John Williams' score for the film, with its alternating musical notes, E and F, without feeling threatened.

▲ In Disney's *Finding Nemo*, the clownfish Marlin overcomes various dangers during his search for his son, Nemo, including a trio of sharks. Bruce, the great white, has pledged — with great difficulty — to give up eating fish. His companions are a winghead hammerhead called Anchor and a mako called Chum.

▶ Few works of art stop people in their tracks like this one. The English artist Damien Hirst's infamous *The Physical Impossibility of Death in the Mind of Someone Living* was unveiled to the public in 1991. It is a glass case containing the carcass of a tiger shark preserved in a liquid chemical called formaldehyde.

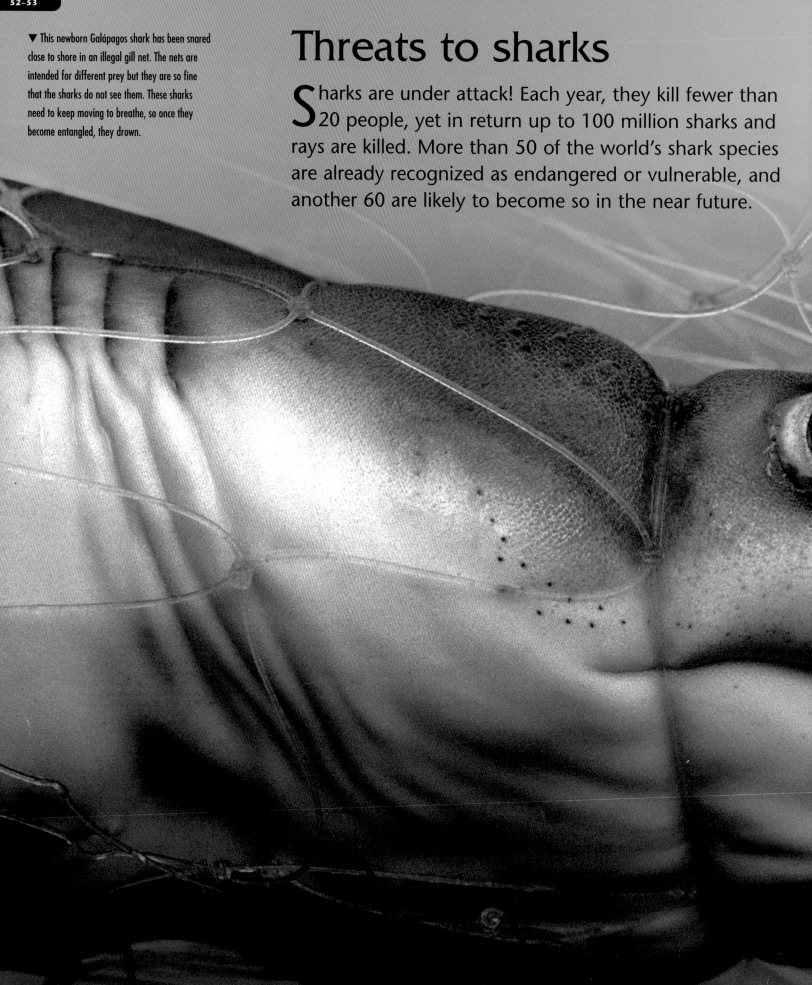

▼ This newborn Galápagos shark has been snared close to shore in an illegal gill net. The nets are intended for different prey but they are so fine that the sharks do not see them. These sharks need to keep moving to breathe, so once they become entangled, they drown.

Threats to sharks

Sharks are under attack! Each year, they kill fewer than 20 people, yet in return up to 100 million sharks and rays are killed. More than 50 of the world's shark species are already recognized as endangered or vulnerable, and another 60 are likely to become so in the near future.

▲ Shark-fin soup is a delicacy in Japan and China. In Hong Kong, a single dorsal fin from a whale shark or basking shark can fetch the equivalent of around £10,000. Fishermen simply cut off the fin and throw the living shark back into the water to die.

Sharks for sale

People fish sharks for sport and food; they make leather from their skins and medicines from their cartilage; and they harvest squalene oil from their livers. They make their teeth into jewellery and sell jaws as souvenirs. As well as the sharks that are deliberately fished, there are accidental bycatches – sharks caught in nets intended for other fish. However, by far the largest number of deaths are because of finning – cutting off the fins for shark-fin soup.

Habitat destruction

Shark habitats are also under threat. Detergents, pesticides and other chemicals are flushed into waterways and enter the sea, where they are absorbed by sharks and their prey. The toxins kill sharks and damage their unborn young. Land development can be another problem. On Bimini in the Bahamas, for example, the lemon shark's mangrove breeding grounds have been bulldozed to build a resort, causing the survival rate to fall 30 per cent in 11 years.

▲ Dead sharks caught by game fishermen trail behind a boat off the coast of Florida, USA. Game fishermen hunt sharks for sport and collect the jaws as trophies. Game fishing may reduce the shark population in a small locality, but it is not as serious a threat to sharks as bycatching and finning.

Getting up close

If the threats to sharks are to be reduced, then people need to discover more about the species they are trying to save. The best way to find out about an animal is to spend time watching it closely in its habitat. Observing the faster and more dangerous sharks has obvious risks, so shark-watchers and scientists have devised different ways to protect themselves.

Divers in armour

Ron Taylor is the Australian shark photographer who shot the live shark sequences for the film *Jaws*. He came up with the idea of diving in a protective, metal mesh suit. In 1979 his wife, fellow shark expert Valerie, tested one out on grey reef sharks. The suit works with smaller sharks, but would offer no protection against a great white.

▲ A diver attaches a Shark Shield™ to his leg. This device sends out electronic signals that target the ampullae of Lorenzini (see pages 36–37) around a shark's snout. As the shark approaches the device, the signals become more and more uncomfortable and eventually the shark turns and swims away.

◀ Valerie Taylor successfully tests a lightweight version of the original stainless-steel mesh suit against the bite of a whitetip reef shark, off the coast of Australia. This suit has helped the Taylors study in depth how sharks bite and how they feed.

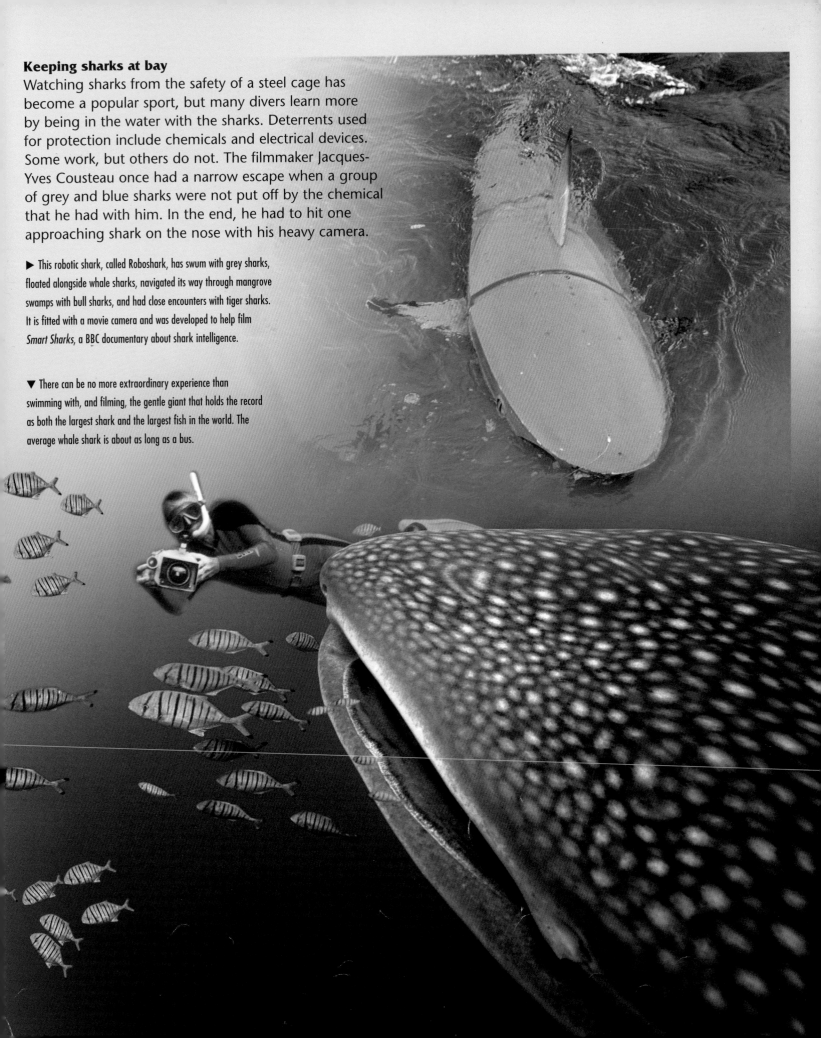

Keeping sharks at bay

Watching sharks from the safety of a steel cage has become a popular sport, but many divers learn more by being in the water with the sharks. Deterrents used for protection include chemicals and electrical devices. Some work, but others do not. The filmmaker Jacques-Yves Cousteau once had a narrow escape when a group of grey and blue sharks were not put off by the chemical that he had with him. In the end, he had to hit one approaching shark on the nose with his heavy camera.

▶ This robotic shark, called Roboshark, has swum with grey sharks, floated alongside whale sharks, navigated its way through mangrove swamps with bull sharks, and had close encounters with tiger sharks. It is fitted with a movie camera and was developed to help film *Smart Sharks*, a BBC documentary about shark intelligence.

▼ There can be no more extraordinary experience than swimming with, and filming, the gentle giant that holds the record as both the largest shark and the largest fish in the world. The average whale shark is about as long as a bus.

Conservation

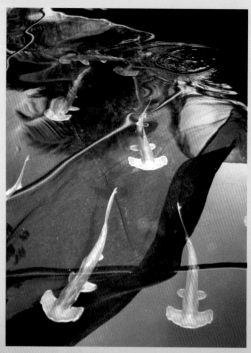

Threatened shark species urgently need help. In the last 15 years alone, numbers of hammerheads and great whites have reduced by 70 per cent worldwide. One way to protect sharks is to learn more about them. Scientists and conservationists use accurate research to educate people. They also persuade governments to help, for example by outlawing finning and tackling pollution.

◀ In Kaneohe Bay, Hawaii, marine biologists have been tagging scalloped hammerhead pups. They now know that between 5,000 and 10,000 pups are born in the bay each year. This kind of research helps scientists to protect shark habitats.

► This acoustic transmitter has been used to track the movements and behaviour of basking sharks at their summer feeding grounds in the Irish Sea. The transmitter sends out pulses of sound that are picked up by a receiver on the research vessel.

Laws to protect sharks

More than 60 countries have banned finning (see page 53), but not all of them have the resources to enforce the law. In 2003, some 300,000 shark fins were exported from Ecuador to China and Hong Kong for shark-fin soup. Then Ecuador banned finning – but the industry is still thriving. The country does not have enough money to police shark fishing effectively.

Taking action

Conservation organizations and marine biologists study sharks in the wild and pass on information about how sharks can be helped. They also try to correct misinformation. For example, many people still believe that sharks are immune to tumours and that squalene from their liver oil can protect people against cancers. By showing that this is a myth, scientists may be able to stop people from killing so many sharks for their oil.

◄ In the Coral Sea, off the northeast coast of Australia, two scientists attach a tag to a whitetip reef shark's tail. The tag will record the temperature and depth of the water in which the shark swims and send the data to the scientists' receiving device.

SUMMARY OF CHAPTER 3: SHARKS AND PEOPLE

Sharks through the ages

Throughout human history, sharks have been revered and feared. They have been worshiped as gods, taken center stage in religious ceremonies and rituals, and influenced the actions of many traditional peoples worldwide. They have also played starring roles in movies and books and have made personal appearances in works of art.

Death threat

Many sharks are endangered or under threat of extinction. This is partly because they are hunted and killed by people for food or sport or drowned in nets intended for other fish. Almost 550 species of sharks and rays are thought to be in some sort of danger, more than 100 of which are threatened with extinction. If people do not change their actions—for example, if demand for shark-fin soup continues—this list will only get longer.

Saving the shark

People can change the future of sharks. To begin with, they can find out more about sharks and contact conservation organizations. They can campaign to stop overfishing and for the reduction in the enormous number of deaths caused through by-catching. They can ban shark-fin soup and avoid shark meat unless it comes from managed fisheries. And they can make sure that any products that they buy, including jewelry, cosmetics, and leather, do not come from sharks.

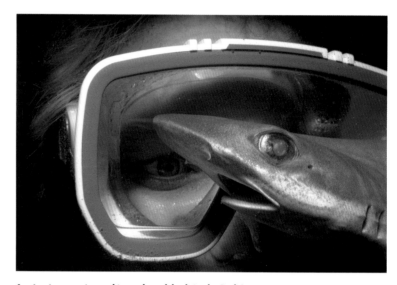

A scientist examines a bigeye houndshark in the Red Sea.

Go further . . .

Discover how you can help protect sharks: www.bbc.co.uk/nature/animals/conservation/sharks/

Make a difference at the Bite-Back site: www.bite-back.com

The Shark Trust gives information about shark education and campaigns: www.sharktrust.org

Animals Under Threat: Great White Shark by Louise and Richard Spilsbury (Heinemann Library, 2004)

Informania: Sharks by Christopher Maynard (Candlewick, 2000)

Conservationist
Someone who works to preserve nature and the environment.

Marine biologist
A scientist who specializes in marine ecology.

Researcher
Someone who studies a subject closely so that they can present it in a detailed and accurate way.

Specialist
A scientist who becomes an expert in one subject or part of a subject.

Learn about shark-diving adventures departing from San Diego, CA, at: Shark Diver
Phone: (415) 404-6144
www.sharkdiver.com

Go basking-shark watching in their summer feeding grounds off the U.K.'s southwestern coast:
Elemental Tours
Cornwall, U.K.
Phone: +44 (0) 1736 811 200
www.elementaltours.co.uk

See sharks in a tropical lagoon habitat at Nausicaa sea life center:
Boulevard Sainte Beuve
62200 Boulogne-sur-Mer, France
Phone: +33 (3) 21 30 98 98
www.nausicaa.fr/Anglais/accveil.htm

Glossary

ampullae (singular: ampulla) of Lorenzini
Jelly-filled pits in the skin of a shark's head that allow it to detect electric signals emitted by other animals.

amulet
A small object worn as a protective charm.

anal fin
A single fin on the stomach between the pelvic and caudal fins of some sharks.

asymmetric
Unbalanced, not of equal length.

baitball
A ball-shaped mass of fish prey herded together.

barbel
One of two long, whisker-like lobes on the snouts of some sharks, which help to find prey through touch and taste.

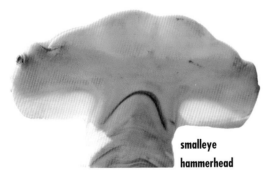

smalleye hammerhead

benthic
Bottom-dwelling.

bioluminescent
Giving out a light produced by living organisms.

bony fish
Any fish with a skeleton made of bone rather than cartilage.

breaching
Leaping out of the water and splashing back in.

buoyant
Able to float in water. The squalene oil in a shark's liver helps it to float, because it is much lighter than water.

bycatch
Unwanted fish taken by accident when fishing for a particular species.

camouflage
Markings on the body of an animal that help it to blend in with its background.

cartilage
A lightweight, flexible material that makes up the skeleton of a shark.

caudal fin
The fin on the tail of a shark that carries the end of the spinal column.

chimaera
A smooth-skinned, cartilaginous fish related to skates and rays.

conservation
Looking after animals, plants and natural resources so that they do not become extinct or run out.

copepod
A small crustacean often found among zooplankton.

coral
Rock formed from the external skeletons of tiny sea creatures called polyps, that piles up to form a reef.

crustacean
An animal without a backbone, but with a hard shell and a segmented body. Crabs, shrimps, copepods and barnacles are all crustaceans.

shark amulet

denticle
A small, tooth-like scale on the skin of a shark.

dorsal fin
A shark's main fin, located on its back between the head and the caudal fin.

ecology
The scientific study of how living things relate to each other.

ecosystem
A living community of different species that interact.

ectothermic
Cold-blooded, having a body temperature that rises and falls to match the temperature outside.

electrosensory perception
The ability to detect electric signals given out by other animals.

embryo
A developing young animal before it has been born or hatched.

endothermic
Warm-blooded, having a body temperature that stays warm whatever the temperature is outside.

extinct
Describes an animal or plant species that has died out completely.

feeding frenzy
When a group of sharks attack prey and become very aggressive and excited by the blood in the water.

filter-feeding
An eating method used by some
sharks that involves using the
gill-rakers to strain plankton
and small fish from the water.

finning
Cutting off a shark's fin and then
throwing the body back in the sea.

food chain
The flow of energy from one living
thing to another in a particular
environment. Predators such as sharks
are at the top of the food chain.

fossil
The preserved remains of an animal
or plant.

gill
An opening on the side or underside
of the head of a shark or ray that is
used for breathing. Most sharks have
five or seven pairs of gills.

gill-raker
A comb-like part of the gills of
some sharks that is used to filter
food from the water.

dogfish
egg case

habitat
The environment in
which an animal lives.

invertebrate
Having no backbone.

larva (plural: larvae)
A young animal that changes its
shape as it grows up.

lateral line
A system of fluid-filled channels that
run from the head along the sides
of a shark's body. These detect tiny
movements of prey and vibrations
in the water.

mammal
An animal with a backbone whose
young feed on their mother's milk.

metabolize
To use the metabolism (the physical
and chemical systems that keep an
animal or plant alive) to change
something, such as food into energy.

migration
The seasonal movement of animals
from one place to another in search
of food or a mate, or to give birth.

mollusc
An animal without a backbone and
with an unsegmented body, usually
protected by a hard shell. Mussels,
snails, clams and squid are molluscs.

nictitating membrane
A moveable extra eyelid that protects
the eyes of some sharks from damage
when they attack.

nocturnal
Active at night.

blue shark

ocellus
An eyespot.

oviparous
Describes an animal that lays eggs.

ovoviviparous
Describes an animal that produces eggs that develop and hatch inside the mother's body.

pectoral fin
One of a pair of fins on a shark that are on each side of its body just behind the head.

pelagic
Describes sharks of the open ocean.

pelvic fin
One of a pair of fins on a shark that are on each side of its body between its stomach and tail.

photophore
A small, dark spot that can produce light, found on the bodies of some sharks, such as lanternsharks.

plankton
Tiny animals and plants, often microscopic, that float near the surface of the sea.

pollution
Harmful substances and waste that poison the environment.

predator
An animal that hunts and eats another animal.

prey
An animal that is hunted by another, usually larger, animal.

ray
A flat-bodied, cartilaginous fish related to sharks and similar to a skate, except it produces live young.

sawfish
A flat-bodied, cartilaginous fish related to sharks, that has a long, sawlike snout.

skate
A flat-bodied, cartilaginous fish related to sharks and similar to a ray, except it lays eggs.

species
A group of animals or plants that have similar characteristics and are able to breed among themselves.

spiral valve
Corkscrew-shaped folds in a shark's intestine that help to slow digestion.

squalene
An oil present in the liver of sharks.

swim bladder
An air-filled sac in many fish that helps them keep buoyant.

tag
To attach a marker or label to a shark's skin to track its movements.

temperate
Describes places between the tropics and poles, where there are seasons.

tropical
Describes places near the Equator, where it is hot all year round.

vertebrate
Having a backbone.

viviparous
Describes an animal that produces young that develop inside the mother's body.

zooplankton
Animal plankton.

Galápagos shark

Index

aboriginal people 48
acoustic transmitters 57
Alvin 28
Amazon river 24, 41
ampullae of Lorenzini 18, 21, 29, 36, 37, 46, 54, 59
anatomy 10
angel sharks 8, 31, 45

baitballs 38, 39, 59
barbels 36, 45, 59
basking sharks 9, 42, 43
benthic sharks 32, 44–45, 59
  see also bottom feeders
bioluminescence 10, 43, 59
blood 6, 37, 39, 40, 41, 59
blue sharks 11, 12, 24, 26, 46, 61
bluntnose sharks 29
bones 8, 10
bottom-dwelling sharks *see* benthic sharks
bottom-feeders 10, 31, 44–45
  see also benthic sharks
brain 10
breathing 10, 52, 60
bull sharks 24, 25, 40, 41
bycatching 53, 58, 59

camouflage 9, 21, 23, 44, 45, 59
Carcharhiniformes 8
carpet sharks 8, 30
cartilage 8, 10, 11, 14, 15, 22, 53, 59, 61
catsharks 12, 37, 45
chimaera 23, 59
cold-blooded sharks *see* ectothermic sharks
conservation 41, 52–53, 56–57, 58
cookiecutter sharks 10, 28, 35
copepods 20, 42, 59
copper sharks 38, 39
coral reefs 9, 31, 59
Cousteau, Jacques-Yves 55
crabs 8, 21, 22, 23, 30, 42, 44, 45
crustaceans 19, 28, 30, 35, 42, 45, 59

cuttlefish 44

deep-sea sharks 28–29
denticles 9, 59
digestion 10, 11, 61
dinosaurs 7
divers 40, 41, 46, 47, 54, 55
dogfish 13, 16, 29, 60
dolphins 29, 35, 38
duodenum 10

ectothermic sharks 27, 59
eggs 12, 13, 61
electricity 23, 36, 46
electrosensory perception 36, 59
electrosensory pits *see* ampullae of Lorenzini
embryos 12, 13, 59
endangered sharks 20–21, 22, 47, 56, 57, 58
endothermic sharks 27, 59
estuaries 7, 19
eyelids, inner *see* nicititating membranes
eyes 8, 19, 20, 29, 30, 34, 37, 39, 45

family tree 8
filter-feeders 17, 42–43, 46, 60
finning 53, 56, 57, 60
fins 8, 9, 11, 14, 18, 23, 26, 30, 45, 53
  anal 9, 59
  caudal 9, 30, 59
  dorsal 9, 14, 23, 30, 59
  pectoral 8, 9, 18, 22, 45, 61
  pelvic 9, 61
food 10, 24, 25, 28, 29, 33, 34, 38, 42–43, 46, 47, 60
fossils 14, 15, 21, 35, 59
Fox, Rodney 41
frilled sharks 8, 29

Galápagos sharks 28, 30, 47, 52, 61
gall bladders 10
game fishing 53
Ganges river 41

gestation 13
gill arches 10, 19, 42
gill-rakers 10, 34, 42, 43, 60
gill slits 8, 9, 22
glossopetrae 14
goblin sharks 21
gods 48, 49, 58
Great Barrier Reef 39, 42
great white sharks 9, 10, 13, 20, 25, 33, 35, 40, 41, 50, 51
Greeks, ancient 48
Greenland sharks 20, 28

habitat destruction 21, 53
hammerheads 6, 8, 12, 18–19, 51, 56, 59
head shapes 18, 19
heart 10
Helicoprion 15
Hemingway, Ernest 50
Heterodontiformes 8
Hexanchiformes 8
Hirst, Damien 51
horn sharks 12
human sacrifices 48
hunting 26, 27, 38–39, 46

ichthyologists 32
International Shark Attack File 40, 41, 46

jaws 15, 17, 19, 21, 29, 33, 34, 35, 45
Jaws (the film) 6, 50, 51, 54
Jonah 48

kelp forests 35
kidneys 11
krill 17

Lamniformes 8
lanternsharks 28, 29
lateral lines 36, 37, 46, 60
legends *see* myths and legends
lemon sharks 12, 13, 35, 53

lifespans 16
Linnaeus 32
litters 13, 17
livers 10, 11, 17, 53, 61

mako sharks 16, 17, 43, 51, 55
man-eating sharks 40–41, 50
mangroves 30, 53, 55
marine biologists 57, 58
marlin 26, 50
medicines 47, 53
Megalodon 14, 35
megamouths 43
mermaids' purses 12
microbiologists 46
migration 24–25, 60
migration, vertical 24, 29
Moho 48
molluscs 30, 31, 35, 45, 60
mouths 8, 29, 30, 42, 43, 45
myths and legends 48–49, 57

naturalists 32
nets 47, 52, 53, 58
nictitating membranes 8, 34, 39, 60
Nohi-Abassi 48
nurse sharks 10, 34, 35, 39, 45
nursery grounds 13
nutrients 10, 12

oceanic whitetip sharks 7, 26, 27, 39
oceanographers 46
open-water sharks *see* pelagic sharks
Orectolobiformes 8
Orinoco river 48
Orion 48
overfishing 21, 22
oviparity 12, 61
ovoviviparity 12, 13, 61
oxygen 9, 10, 12

palaeontologists 32
palaeontology 14
parasites 20
pelagic sharks 26, 32, 61
pelvic opening 11
photophores 28, 43, 61
placentas 12, 13
plankton 8, 24, 42, 43, 61

poison 22, 23, 47
Polo, Marco 49
porbeagles 16
predators 8, 14, 19, 22, 23, 27, 28, 32, 33, 44, 45, 61
prehistoric sharks 14–15, 35
pressure sensors 36
prey 8, 9, 18, 21, 22, 23, 29, 31, 31, 34, 39, 40, 43, 45, 46, 61
Pristiophoriformes 8
pups 12, 13, 17, 33
pygmy sharks 16

rays 18, 22–23, 61
reef sharks 9, 30–31, 36, 39, 54, 57
remoras 43
reproduction 12–13, 47
researchers 58
rivers 7, 24, 25, 41, 48
Roboshark 55
Rondelet, Guillaume 48

Samehito 48
sand tiger sharks 13, 30
satellites 24
sawsharks 21
scales 9, 14
Scapanorhyncus 21
scientists 8, 27, 35, 46, 54, 56, 57
seals 33, 35
senses 8, 18, 20, 29, 36–37, 46
sensory cells 36
shark attacks 6, 7, 25, 33, 40–41, 46
shark charmers 49
shark-fin soup 53, 57, 58, 59
shark-kissing ceremony 49
Shark Shield™ 54
shark sizes 8, 16–17
shark watching 54–55, 58
shellfish 10, 21, 22
shells 12, 13, 35
skates 22–23, 61
skeletons 8, 10, 11, 22
skin 9, 22, 31, 45
sleep 8
smoothhound sharks 35
Sphyrnidae family 18
Spielberg, Steven 51
spleen 11

squalene 11, 53, 57, 61
Squaliformes 8
Squatiniformes 8
squid 17, 21, 28, 29, 31, 35, 44, 46, 60
Steno, Nicolas 14
Stethacanthus 14
stomach 11
submersibles 28
suction-feeding 43
surfers 40, 41
swellsharks 35
swim bladders 11, 61
swimmers 40, 41
Systema Naturae 32

tagging 24, 25, 56, 61
tails 9, 10, 11, 22, 23, 26, 27, 28, 46
Taylor, Ron 6, 54
Taylor, Valerie 6, 54
teeth 6, 7, 9, 14, 15, 33, 34–35, 43, 46
temperatures 27, 28, 57
tenguzame 21
tentacles 44
thresher sharks 26, 27
tiger sharks 10, 13, 24, 35, 39, 40, 41, 49, 50, 51
Tlingit tribe 49
tongue stones *see glossopatrae*
tropical islands 30

uterus 11, 12, 13

viviparity 12, 61

Warao Indians 48
warm-blooded sharks *see* endothermic sharks
warning signs 40
whale sharks 16, 17, 43, 55
Williams, John 51
wobbegong sharks 8, 12, 44

Zambezi river 41
zebra bullhead sharks 8, 31, 35, 45
zebra sharks 31
zoologists 32
zooplankton 42, 43, 61

Acknowledgements

The publisher would like to thank the following for permission to reproduce their material. Every care has been taken to trace copyright holders. However, if there have been unintentional omissions or failure to trace copyright holders, we apologize and will, if informed, endeavour to make corrections in any future edition.

Key: *b* = bottom, *c* = centre, *l* = left, *r* = right, *t* = top, *bg* = background

Cover *c* Gary Bell/Oceanwide Images; *bg* Amos Nachoum/Corbis; Page 1 Alamy/Jeff Rotman; 2–3 Seapics/Bob Cranston; 4–5 Seapics/Phillip Colla; 7 Frank Lane Picture Agency (FLPA)/Norbert Wu; 8–9*t* Ardea/Valerie Taylor; 8–9*b* Seapics/Doug Perrine; 9*tr* Seapics/Doug Perrine; 9*cr* Seapics/D.D. Schrischte; 9*br* Seapics/Jonathan Bird; 11*b* Seapics/David B. Fleetham; 12*b* Seapics/Mark Conlin; 13*t* Nature/Jeff Rotman; 15*c* Seapics/Doug Perrine; 15*br* Seapics/Bob Cranston; 16*tl* Alamy/Ace Stock Limited; 16*tl* FLPA/Minden Pictures; 16–17*c* Seapics/Garry Bell; 17*tr* Seapics/Richard Herrmann; 17*br* Seapics/Manfred Bail; 18–19*bg* Seapics/Paul Humann; 18 Seapics/James D. Watt; 19 Seapics/Stephen Kajiura; 20–21 Nature Picture Library/Doug Perrine; 21*t* Seapics/David Shen; 21*b* Seapics/Doug Perrine; 22–23*t* Nature Picture Library/Doug Perrine; 22*b* Nature Picture library/Jeff Rotman; 23 Seapics/Jeff Jaskolski; 24 Alamy/Mike Greenslade; 25*t* Seapics/Doug Perrine; 25*b* Seapics/James D. Watt; 26–27*t* Seapics/Richard Herrmann; 26*b* Seapics/Amos Nachoum; 27*b* Seapics/Masa Ushioda; 28*tl* Getty Images/Time & Life Pictures/Henry Groskinsky; 30*c* Photolibrary.com; 30*b* Nature Picture Library/Brandon Cole; 31*r* Getty/Imagebank; 31*b* Photolibrary.com; 32 Seapics/Doug Perrine; 33 Photolibrary.com; 34 Seapics/Jeff Rotman; 35*tl* Corbis/Louie Psihoyos; 35*bl* Nature Picture Library/Jeff Rotman; 35*br* Getty/National Geographic Society; 36–37*t* Photolibrary.com; 36*b* Seapics/Doug Perrine; 38 Seapics/Doug Perrine; 39*tr* Seapics/Jeff Rotman; 39*b* Seapics/Ron & Valerie Taylor; 40–41 Alamy/Stephen Frink Collection; 40*l* Science Photo Library; 41*t* Alamy/Bruce Coleman; 42 Nature Picture Library/Alan James; 43*tl* Seapics/Peter Parks/iq3-d; 43*cr* Photolibrary.com; 44–45*t* Seapics/A&A Ferrari; 44*b* Ardea/Valerie Taylor; 46 Seapics/Bob Cranston; 47 Seapics/Masa Ushioda; 48 Alamy/Visual&Written SL; 48–49 Art Archive/Biblioteca Nacional Lisboa; 49*t* PA Archive; 49*b* Corbis/Canadian Museum of Civilization; 50*cl* Corbis; 50–51 AKG/Disney Enterprises; 51*t* AKG/Universal Pictures; 51*b* Corbis/James Leynse; 52–53 FLPA/Minden Pictures; 53*t* Seapics/Masa Ushioda; 53*b* FLPA/Minden Pictures; 54 Ardea/Valerie Taylor; 54*c* Sharkshield.com, Australia; 55*t* Nature Picture Library/Peter Kragh; 55*b* Ardea/Valerie Taylor; 56*tl* Seapics/Andy Seale; 56–57*b* Nature Picture Library/Jurgen Freund; 57*t* Corbis/Jeff Rotman; 58 Seapics/Jeff Rotman; 59*bl* Seapics/Doug Perrine; 59*tr* Werner Forman Archive; 60–61*t* Seapics/Masa Ushioda; 60*bl* Photolibrary.com; 61*br* Photolibrary.com; 62–63 Photolibrary.com; 64 Seapics/C&M Fallows.

The publisher would like to thank the following illustrators:
Ray Grinaway 45; Sebastian Quigley (Linden Artists) 14–15; Sam Weston and Steve Weston (Linden Artists) 28–29; Steve Weston (Linden Artists) 10–11, 12–13; Peter Winfield 8, 10, 19, 24–25, 36, 37, 43.